The National Transportation Systems Center

U.S. Department of Transportation
Research and Innovative Technology Administration

Proceedings of the Workshop on
Human Response to Aviation Noise in Protected Natural Areas

Volpe National Transportation Systems Center
Cambridge, MA
October 28-29, 2008

Table of Contents

1.0   Introduction

The Federal Aviation Administration (FAA), Western Pacific Region, Office of Special Programs sponsored this workshop, with assistance from the FAA, Office of Environment and Energy, and the National Park Service (NPS) Office of Soundscape Research. The workshop was hosted by the Research and Innovative Technology Administration's Volpe National Transportation Systems Center.

The workshop brought together experts in the fields of engineering acoustics, social science, psychology, and recreation management in order to identify important research topics that will inform FAA and NPS as they develop a plan to advance understanding of aircraft noise effects on park visitors.

2.0   Purpose of the Workshop

According to Section 808 of the National Parks Air Tour Management Act of 2000, any methodology adopted by a Federal agency to assess air tour noise in any unit of the national park system shall be based on reasonable scientific methods. Therefore, the FAA and NPS share a mutual interest to develop scientifically defensible methodology to quantitatively assess noise impacts from aviation in National Parks. Although the agencies could pursue wholly independent research programs, public investment in research will realize the highest return if the FAA and NPS mutually develop a prioritized list of research topics and a coordinated strategy for stimulating this research.

To date, several studies have been funded by these agencies which strive to define the relationship between aircraft noise "dose" and an associated human response (dose-response) gathered from park visitor surveys.[1, 2, 3, 4] Following the example of residential dose-response relationships, the analyses of the data from the park visitor studies focused on evaluating relatively simple functional forms of noise doses and mediating variables as predictors of visitor responses in surveys. However, research results suggest that a simple model does not adequately characterize human responses to noise in protected natural and cultural areas, such as National Parks. In addition to visitor responses to noise as measured by annoyance or acceptability, research is needed to investigate physiological responses to noise events and the degree to which noise degrades opportunities to perceive the sounds of the park.

3.0   List of Participants

Technical Experts:
Grant Anderson, Independent Consultant
Bill Borrie, PhD, University of Montana
James Fields, PhD, Independent Consultant
Richard Horonjeff, Independent Consultant
Steve Lawson, PhD, Resource Systems Group / Virginia Technological University
Britton Mace, PhD, Southern Utah University (via phone)
Robert Manning, PhD, University of Vermont
Nicholas Miller, HMMH Inc.

[1] Anderson, et. al., Dose-Response Relationships Derived From Data Collected at Grand Canyon, Haleakala and Hawaii Volcanoes National Parks, NPOA Report No. 93-6, National Park Service, Denver Colorado 80225, October 1993.

[2] Fleming, et. al., Development of Noise Dose/Visitor Response Relationships for the National Parks Overflight Rule: Bryce Canyon National Park Study, Report No. FAA-AEE-98-01, US Department of Transportation, Washington DC 20591, July 1998.

[3] Miller, et. al., Mitigating the Effects of Military Aircraft Overflights on Recreational Users of Parks, HMMH Report No. 294470.04, HMMH Inc., Burlington, MA, 1999.

[4] Rapoza, et. al., Study of Visitor Response to Air Tour and Other Aircraft Noise in National Parks, Report No. DTS-34-FA65-LR1, US Department of Transportation, Cambridge MA 02142, January 2005.

FAA Representatives:
Barry Brayer, Office of Special Programs, Western-Pacific Region
Pete Ciesla, Office of Special Programs, Western-Pacific Region
Keith Lusk Office of Special Programs, Western-Pacific Region
Raquel Girvin, PhD, Office of Environment and Energy, Headquarters
Bill He, PhD, Office of Environment and Energy, Headquarters
Rebecca Cointin, Office of Environment and Energy, Headquarters
Jake Plante, EdD, Office of Airport Plans and Programming, Headquarters

NPS Representatives:
Kurt Fristrup, PhD, Natural Sounds Program Office, Ft. Collins
Frank Turina, Natural Sounds Program Office, Ft. Collins
Rick Ernenwein, Grand Canyon National Park
Shan Burson, Grand Teton National Park

Volpe Center Representatives:
Paul Valihura, PhD, Workshop Organizer
Amanda Rapoza, Workshop Organizer
Rachael Barolsky, Moderator
Adam Klauber, Note-Taker
Gregg Fleming
Cynthia Lee

Observers:
Alan Stephen National Parks Overflight Advisory Group (NPOAG) member representing Fixed-Wing Air Tour Operators
Greg Price, Consultant for Alan Stephen
Bryan Faehner, NPOAG member alternate representing National Parks Conservation Association
Philip Mattson, Volpe
John McGuiggin, Volpe
Frank Smigelski, Volpe
Jennifer Papazian, Volpe

4.0   Workshop Structure

The goals of the workshop were to foster interdisciplinary identification of unresolved scientific questions regarding the effects of aircraft noise on park visitors, and to emerge with a prioritized list of research topics and estimates of the level of support needed to make progress on each topic. Interdisciplinary discussions are most productive when participants develop shared insights regarding each other's domains. The proposed structure of the workshop sought to foster discussions among scientists and federal managers who might not routinely interact.

The first day of the workshop consisted of concise (15-minute) presentations by each participant to the entire group, arranged in Sessions by shared disciplines or research themes. Each participant was required to conclude his or her presentation with recommendations for future research. During the opening remarks, participants were informed of FAA perspectives and given a summary of the noise-exposure / human response research that has been conducted to date. Session I contained presentations to inform the participants further on NPS perspectives and related human dimensions of soundscape research. Session II contained presentations to address some of the known gaps in the current noise exposure / human response research and ideas to achieve resolution. At the conclusion of each Session, 20-30 minutes of discussion followed to resolve questions. The day concluded with an

hour of discussions in breakout groups. The participants were divided into three intentionally heterogeneous teams that discussed the research topics that would be of greatest value.

The second day consisted of further discussion to develop a clear set of next-steps and a path to move forward. These discussions centered on "What questions can be answered with the current exposure/response data?", and "What questions can not be answered with the current exposure/response data?" The next-steps for each agency (summarized in Section 6) were based on these discussions.

A moderator was used to facilitate and manage the discussions. This format provided equal consideration for each participant's contributions. The workshop products provide the FAA and NPS with information about the breadth of support for various research topics and the diversity of opinion regarding the value and cost of each topic. Neither agency nor the participants were required to make concluding statements or commitments to particular plans.

5.0   Summary of Individual Participant Recommendations and Discussion Themes

The research recommendations, which were included in each participant's presentation, have been merged within topic areas and summarized in the following section. In addition, a number of general themes emerged from the workshop discussions that provide a useful context for thinking about the next steps outlined in Section 7. These recommendation and discussion themes are as follows:

Management and Decision-Making:
FAA and NPS both agree that noise impacts on a park's natural soundscape must be assessed. Visitor exposure-response relationships offer a potential basis for establishing metrics and thresholds to analyze noise impacts in National Parks. The FAA believes strongly that the assessment should be consistent from park to park. However, the NPS is decentralized in nature, as many decisions are made either at the park or at the regional level. The decentralized decision-making process at individual parks, combined with the huge variation in resources across National Park units, makes it challenging to adopt general guidelines regarding noise impacts on visitors. Nevertheless, researchers emphasized the benefits of pre-determined National Park management goals related to park resource / management areas.

Researchers stress that FAA / NPS policy-makers will need to determine the impact thresholds. Science will only reveal the underlying relationships that can serve as a basis for decision-making. It may be helpful for decision-makers to physically participate in acoustic measurement activities or site visits. Without these site visits, it will be difficult to understand the metrics and make sound policy decisions.

Findings from Past Research:
Visitors consistently cite natural quiet as a factor for visitation and aircraft noise as a detractor from the experience. They may decide not to visit a park due to soundscape degradation. Visitors are generally highly supportive of management actions; these actions might be used in the future to alter visitor behavior and expectations.

General Recommendations for Future Efforts:
There is value in returning to the already compiled dose-response data to conduct more analysis. As a starting point, the existing noise dose-response data should be further mined. This analysis should include an evaluation of the context of the data (e.g., visitor populations, park setting, noise source and type of NPS unit). The results should be jointly reviewed & policy implications re-visited. The re-analysis should be used to derive estimates of response variation to use for future study designs (site, day, group, effects).

 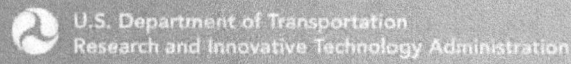

A systematic approach to future research should be used. This approach would ideally combine both engineering and sociological research methods and involve regular consultation with Federal agencies. It was suggested that research related to the concept of "solitude" might provide a framework for the research progression for "natural quiet" and noise impacts on visitors, especially those to backcountry / wilderness locations.

Recommendations for Future data Collection Efforts:
Any future studies involving data collection should be designed to address one or more of the following factors:
1) Noise-sensitive visitor categories such as wilderness or backcountry visitors.
2) Response indicators beyond annoyance. National Park managers are managing to create outstanding experiences. Measuring negative reactions may not be helpful for park managers.
3) The influence of other anthropogenic sources (snow-machines, personal watercraft, high-altitude jets, traffic, etc.) on overall visitor experience.
4) How parks and park soundscapes are perceived and experienced by visitors. Questions such as "What values & meanings are most important?", "What it the relationship of natural sounds to other aspects of experience of parks?", "Should different natural soundscapes should be managed differently?", "Do visitors evaluate experience based on soundscape?", and "If multiple natural soundscape opportunities exist, is it valuable to inventory them and adopt management policy to protect them? " should be answered.

Measurement sites should be chosen by considering the characteristics of the site such as visitor numbers, visitor activities (sensitivity etc), aircraft and ambient noise environment, and the possibility of observing variations in policy variables within site. Data collection should have precise statistical requirements set by FAA & NPS working individually, together and with consultants considering the actions and policies that will be affected by study results.

Recommendations for alternate research methods:
Lab examination could be used to explore, in a controlled setting, factors which may influence the dose-response relationship. These factors include:
1) The noise dose. Percent time audible, Leq, Lmax, or the number of encounters could be systematically varied.
2) Response scales which move beyond annoyance and/or include wilderness values.
3) The significance of the soundscape(s) or acoustic zone.

Observational methods could also be used to examine visitor response. This could be useful at viewpoints affected by aircraft overflights.

6.0   Overview of Workshop Presentations

The following Section attempts to briefly summarize the major theme of each workshop presentation. Invited experts were not required to prepare a formal paper for distribution. Full copies of the slides from each presentation can be found in Appendix A.

6.1   Opening Remarks

Barry Brayer, Raquel Girvin, and Jake Plante, all from the FAA opened the workshop with remarks intended to inform the workshop participants on their perspectives on aviation noise in National Parks and desires for workshop outcome.

 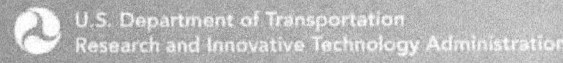
FAA: Special Programs Office (Presentation 0.1)

FAA welcomes all the participants to this workshop and requests contributions in order to build a framework leading to reasonable scientific methods to analyze aircraft impacts at National Parks.

The FAA is working with the National Park Service to implement the National Park Air Tour Management Act of 2000. There are 74 private air tour operators flying over 86 National Park units and 5 abutting tribal lands. Two versions of the Draft Air Tour Management Plan (ATMP) Implementation Plan have been completed to date.

FAA Special Programs Office is the nationwide lead for the ATMP Program and provides support for Grand Canyon Overflights Environmental Impact Statement (EIS). The ATMP programs require cooperation between the FAA and NPS to develop required documentation. Currently, the FAA and NPS are preparing environmental documents for ATMPs at Mount Rushmore National Memorial, Badlands National Park, Haleakala National Park, Hawaii Volcanoes National Park, as well as the EIS for the Grand Canyon Overflights project. For ATMPs, the agencies have differing views on noise metrics, reference ambient data, and impact determinations. An interagency Technical Team has been established to review the proposed NPS framework for evaluating impacts of aircraft noise for use in the Grand Canyon Overflights EIS.

The agencies realize that there are data gaps and one of the main challenges is to develop a technically defensible approach to determine significant noise impacts for aviation-related projects in naturally quiet areas. The FAA Special Programs office is funding a number of research projects through Volpe, with FAA's Office of Environment and Energy as technical lead, to meet this goal. Noise exposure-response relationships are thresholds are regarded as the highest value research program to support ATMPs.

FAA: Aviation Energy and Environment (AEE) (Presentation 0.2)

Noise impact analysis is needed as part of the National Parks ATMPs. Noise impact analyses are also necessary to comply with NEPA for airport and airspace redesign projects. FAA Order 1050.1E cites a number of environmental compliance requirements to study environmental impacts. Within National Parks, FAA and NPS agree that noise impacts on the park's natural soundscape must be assessed. Outside of National Parks, ATMP noise impact analysis will follow standard policies and procedures outlined in FAA Order 1050.1E.

It is understood that the threshold and metric that FAA uses, 65 dBA Day-Night Average Sound Level (DNL), inadequately addresses natural quiet areas in National Parks. Noise in excess of 65 DNL will be considered significant; however, significance beyond NPS "minor" impact descriptors, yet less than 65 DNL, remains to be determined. Visitor exposure-response relationships offer a potential basis for establishing metrics and thresholds to analyze noise impacts in National Parks.

The goal of this workshop is to establish a scientifically defensible approach for measuring and modeling the characteristics of noise exposure that correlate with visitors' evaluation of how noise affects the quality of their environment at different National Parks. The main objective is to develop a roadmap that will advance research and produce a reliable body of data on National Parks and visitors' response to aircraft noise exposure.

At the workshop, the expectation is to establish a common understanding of findings from exposure-response research and data analysis completed to date. In addition, it would be helpful to prioritize key questions that must be answered by follow-on research, and propose and discuss multiple potential paths to answer key questions.

Some questions for the research roadmap:
- Measurement – How can visitor response measurement be improved?

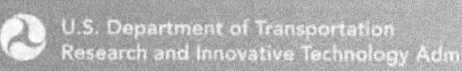

- Variables – Which variables are needed to sufficiently cover the range of desired visitor experiences?
- Metrics – How can the selected metrics be computed and validated?
- Controls – What factors need to be controlled to improve the predictive power of exposure-response models?
- Frequency & Magnitude – Does visitor response vary with less frequent "louder" aircraft vs. more frequent "quieter" aircraft noise?
- Non-acoustic Factors – What factors may affect visitor experience?
- General Park Characteristics – Are there characteristics that can be applied across park units?

The answers to these questions and others will help determine the ultimate metrics, thresholds, and mitigation measures.

FAA: Airports (Prepared comments – full text included in Appendix B)

In its report to the meeting, the FAA Airports Office stated that it has completed several large airport studies involving aircraft noise over parks. Solving aviation-related park noise issues requires a careful balance between aviation and park resource management. The question of compatible land use lies at the heart of these issues. FAA Airports believes that the focus should move away from experimental noise metrics and toward noise criteria: a series of dose-response curves applied to representative park land uses based on management and ambient zoning.

The Airports Office urged under any approach more basic science to improve the applied science and methodology. The main problem today, Airports said, is with the highly experimental audibility metric. In airport studies, audibility over-predictions for cumulative operations have been 400-500 percent above the total time in a day. Project-based calculations also show unrealistic project benefits. Airports also reported its lack of confidence in the so-called "compression algorithm", which is a statistical process of forcing audibility data into a realistic 100 percent scale, and recommended a formal validation study of the audibility metric before it is applied in further studies.

The Airports Office acknowledged that the Day-Night Average Sound Level (DNL) of 65 dB is not compatible for many areas within National Parks. So where can we take some next steps? The Airports Office suggested a few priorities:

1) Focus on the most important human impacts in a park environment (i.e., visitor annoyance), and let other possible impacts wait, such as wildlife.
2) Look at park land use designations and how the NPS and other resource agencies can develop standardized, national guidance in this area.
3) Look at conventional noise metrics that are the most reliable, easy to implement, and cost-effective such as Time Above Ambient (TAA) and LAeq. These metrics came up strong in the dose-response studies and can be readily applied with confidence.
4) Further dose-response work, especially for backcountry assessments.

NPS: Planning Team (Comments - no presentation slides)

NPS representatives provided context regarding air tours and their impact on visitor experience at a few specific parks.

At the Grand Canyon there are many air tours and there has been an extended process to determine how best to manage them. Currently, the working group is moving forward with an Environmental Impact Statement (EIS); there is a range of alternatives and the NPS has selected a preferred alternative. NPS is required to mitigate impacts wherever possible and supposed to categorize impacts into a range of impacts (negligible, minor, moderate, and significant).

The NPS management goal at the Grand Canyon is to restore the natural quiet in 50 percent or more of the park in accordance with the National Parks Overflights Act, which calls for the substantial restoration of the natural quiet and experience of the park. Substantial restoration of natural requires that aircraft not be audible in 50 percent or more of the park for 75 – 100 percent of the flight day. A flight day means during daylight hours. This assessment will be performed for all aircraft flying below 18,000 feet.

Impact analysis is in the early stages at the Grand Canyon. Quiet technology is being considered and may enable some aircraft to qualify for exemptions if certain noise criteria are met. The Grand Canyon technical team formed with eight members looking at the scientific methods to support proposed impact thresholds. Expert panel discussions to assist their review on visitor experience and wildlife impacts have already been conducted.

Denali National Park is exempt from the ATMP process. Park managers have seen a shift in visitor concerns from the weather to aircraft impacts. At Grand Teton National Park, the NPS is part of the ATMP process and in addition, is assessing the challenges related to the large commercial airport located within the boundaries of the park.

Background on Current FAA/NPS Dose-Response Data Part I (Presentation 0.3)
Nick Miller

Mr. Miller began dose-response work in 1991 and other groups have adopted his team's approach. He became familiar with the dose response framework from work with residential communities. His team recognized that parks are "different" sound environments from neighborhoods and normal assessment methods might not be applicable. The first park field team had to modify noise equipment, as most equipment at the time would not capture sound levels below 20 dB. The first dose-response data was collected at Haleakala National Park. Previous work was limited to researchers who recorded how often they could physically hear aircraft within a park. At the time, the field team could gather 1-second A-weighted levels. The survey team used "annoyance" for its qualitative metric as it is used for most transportation communities. Annoyance levels were set at moderately, very, and extremely annoyed. Visitors were provided short questionnaires to minimize completion time.

With the first research, the team had difficulty determining type of aircraft; the equipment could not distinguish so the team also assumed that visitors would also not be able to distinguish. All visitor activity was outdoors to ensure that they did not hear indoor noise that could influence responses. The team used Point Imperial at the Grand Canyon, which allowed them to observe visitors at the location, the duration of the visit, and then interview the visitor.

Short hikes were defined as locations where visitors would have to walk 5-10 minutes. The research team realized that background noise is an important feature because it affects audibility.

There has been a shift in management focus to interference with "natural quiet" instead of interference with "enjoyment." People report that scenery is the first concern and the soundscape is second according to transcripts from congressional hearings.

Other projects were conducted at White Sands where researchers asked the following question – "What if we told people to expect impacts?" The field team created signs that read: "Military aircraft can be regularly seen and heard on this walk." Only 40 percent of visitors saw and remembered the sign. The lesson learned was that if you want visitors to do something, you can't expect them to read or think - you have to help them. If the noise cannot be controlled, at least visitors can be informed and they can adjust their own expectations. In addition, at White Sands the team learned that aircraft traveling together reduces annoyance.

Researchers need policy experts to determine where the threshold is for an impact. It is a policy issue to decide threshold as the data will not necessarily give you the answer. Science will only reveal relationships.

Background on Current FAA/NPS Dose-Response Data Part II (Presentation 0.4)
Amanda Rapoza

Volpe went to Bryce Canyon National Park in 1997 to collect short hike data. Bryce seemed like an ideal site due to its large number of visitors and proximity to aircraft. The team tested numerous additional acoustic descriptors to determine if a better relationship could be developed.

Over 900 data points with good surveys and good noise data were recorded. The new acoustic descriptor "change in exposure" was added. The research team received sound level of data across the entire range for time above "0-100%." Typically, 20% of respondents will report annoyance even with no (zero) acoustic dose. Factors influencing responses included context, visitor time spent in environment, presence of children, large groups, and "repeat" visitors. The team was looking for simplicity. In addition, the team was hoping that national management plans could be developed with dose-response findings.

In 1998 a Volpe research team visited overlook sites within Grand Canyon and Bryce Canyon in an effort to explore different sorts of descriptors for different settings/contexts. The team found that visitors on short hikes from the 1997 study were the more annoyed than visitors to overlooks. Volpe looked at the data points and the types of aircraft in an effort to determine "combined" relationships across sites and parks. Percent time above ambient (%TAA) was determined to be the best performing descriptor. Tour aircraft seemed to cause a higher level of annoyance than high altitude aircraft. The team also looked at the difference in response between first-time visitors and repeat visitors and the duration of the visit. Overlook and short hike sites yielded statistically significant differing results.

What additional information can be mined from the current data? (Presentation 0.5)
Grant Anderson

There is value in returning to the already compiled dose-response data to conduct more analysis. It is not worthwhile to seek data that explains every person's annoyance; rather it is worth looking for the correct percentage of visitors with similar responses.

When the original studies were conducted, the unanticipated costs associated with collecting data reduced the available funding for comprehensive and thorough analysis. Prior research analysis differed by study. It is likely that a reanalysis can be done quickly.

The combined database contains data from the Grand Canyon (2 studies), Haleakala, Hawaii Volcanoes, Bryce Canyon and White Sands. The data exist in an Excel spreadsheet format and can be analyzed with dichotomized logistic regression.

Mr. Anderson recommended improving and expanding the analysis of the existing data by augmenting the doses and mediators. He suggested the following dose improvements: 1) compound the doses allowing more than one into the regression, 2) a dose which combines the percent time audible, and how loud when audible, 3) a dose which differentiates between a low signal to noise ratio and a high signal to noise ratio, 4) a dose that includes fluctuations in aircraft L_{eq} and standard deviation, 5) a dose that ignores "shoulders" – also known as the beginning or end of a visit, 6) a dose using noise-free intervals, 7) considering additional site and visitor mediators, and 8) considering both linear and logarithmic dose scales.

6.2   Session 1

What do Park Managers Need to Effectively Manage Air Tours (Presentation 1.1)
Frank Turina

Mr. Turina placed the current workshop into the broader context of NPS decision making. General NPS Management legislated authority was established by both the Organic Act and the Redwoods Act General Authority. NPS has the sole authority for managing the resources – dichotomy with enjoying the resource, while also protecting simultaneously. The National Park Overflights Act directed FAA and NPS to work together to regulate air tours and assess their impacts.

NPS determines what action is significant vs. non-significant. Management Plans (MP) are NPS guidance documents, and MP 4.9 specifies management priorities for soundscapes. Many times, it is difficult to obtain a good understanding of the variables, and there is also high uncertainty associated. The lack of understanding makes it difficult to determine impacts due to the variation between parks. A few notable variables that contribute to the complexity: 1) appropriate vs. inappropriate uses of a park, 2) types of visitors and visitor experience(s), and 3) NPS management objectives for management zones for each park. NPS is decentralized in nature; many decisions are made either at the park or at the regional level.

NPS uses the Visitor Experience and Resource Protection (VERP) framework to assess and protect visitor experience and resource protection. NPS does consider park visitors on snowmobiles and aircraft passengers as visitors.

NPS values professional judgment and often relies on it to set standards and make decisions. NPS makes decisions based on good science/scholarship, public involvement, and advice or insights from experts. The National Parks Omnibus Management Act of 1998 highlights that professional judgment is part of the decision making process.

Science has a key role informing National Park Service. NPS values objective and transparent research. NPS MP 8.11.2 states that the agency will use the best available science; and MP 2.3.1.4 mandates that decisions have to utilize "good" science. NPS Director's Order (DO) 12, which covers NEPA, mandates that decisions are made based on "good" scientific data. NPS MP 4.1 states in cases of uncertainty the protection of natural resources must predominate. If NPS doesn't understand impacts the agency will err on side of protecting resources.

Human Dimensions of Park Soundscapes: Recent Research and Recommendations for Future
Directions - Part I (Presentation 1.2)
Robert Manning

Robert Manning's presentation covered park and outdoor management frameworks. Park and Outdoor Recreation Management uses accepted frameworks to protect resources. Two recognized frameworks are the "Limits of Acceptable Change" (LAC) and "Visitor Experience and Resource Protection" (VERP). The frameworks create management objectives/desired conditions and associated indicators and standards of quality. Management can then monitor the indicators of quality and apply actions to maintain the standards of quality.

Dr. Manning conducted exposure-response related work in Muir Woods National Monument. Visitors selected sound as a priority and found that "noisy" visitors were the 4th highest ranked annoyance in the study. Aircraft was also cited as an annoyance, but was much lower ranked. To utilize normative methods, a standard had to be established covering visitors desired quality. It was determined that noise at 37 dB is the point at which the soundscape quality becomes marginal.

The surveying team worked with NPS to experiment on different management techniques to reduce soundscape degradation. The team used surveys to assess visitor perceptions for each different

 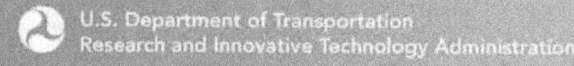

The National Transportation Systems Center — U.S. Department of Transportation Research and Innovative Technology Administration

management action. The management actions included creating quiet zones within the park and "quiet days" with signage requesting visitors to refrain from making loud noises. Visitors were generally highly supportive of management actions.

Past research has been conducted on a site-by-site basis. The work has revealed that visitors appreciate natural sounds and may decide not to visit a park due to soundscape degradation. In the future, it would be useful to create a systemic approach to address the impacts and management approaches based on research.

Human Dimensions of Park Soundscapes: Recent Research and Recommendations for Future Directions - Part II (Presentation 1.3)
Steve Lawson

Dr. Lawson has conducted research at National Parks for more than 10 years. More recently, he connected with the Soundscape Office in 2006 during a NPS workshop. He described recent visitor noise-related work in National Parks and made suggestions for future study.

In the summer of 2007, data was collected at Haleakala National Park (at Kipahulu and within Haleakala Crater) and Hawaii Volcanoes National Park (at Steam Vents and Trail to Thurston Lava Tube). The research method involved an attended listening survey with approximately 30 visitor-based sounds in the inventory. Participants sat for 3-5 minutes and listened (he noted that modern society is virtually unable to sit and listen for more than 30 seconds). Surveyors provided visitors a checklist to check and rate the acceptability of certain sounds in that area of the park. Participants were requested to not only rate acceptability of the sounds, but also make a personal interpretation and rate their feelings/emotions. They were asked for open ended descriptions of any feeling that was associated with the experience. The actual presence or absence of aircraft during the listening exercise was documented by a surveyor.

The visitors noticed helicopters. Visitors, during the study, considered helicopter noise exposure more than once an hour unacceptable. At Haleakala, visitors cited natural quiet as the highest factor for visitation and aircraft noise the highest detractor from the experience.

During this same study, some visitors were outfitted with noise cancelling headphones and played audio clips prepared by Dr. Kurt Fristrup.

Dr. Lawson described the early stage research work at Rocky Mountain National Park to document transportation and user capacity. Using contour mapping, noise modeling, and visitor location (GPS tracks), it is possible to create a predictive simulation showing noise dose.

Future recommendations for National Parks work include the following areas for study:
- Evaluation of context in "dose-response" studies (e.g., visitor populations, setting, noise source and type of NPS unit);
- Measurement of visitor standards for event-based indicators;
- Integration of visitor use and aviation noise modeling;
- Tradeoff analyses of management alternatives;
- In situ studies of soundscape experience & evaluation; and,
- Visual-based assessments of high-altitude flights

Human Dimensions of Park Soundscapes: Recent Research and Recommendations for Future Directions - Part III (Presentation 1.4)
Britton Mace (Called in from external site due to flight cancellation)

Britton Mace began NPS landscape perception work in 1993 and employs experimental social and environmental psychology in laboratory and field studies. One of Dr. Mace's first questions has been

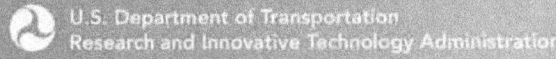
"how can we evaluate different types of landscapes." He has found the recorded sounds can be brought back to research facilities to control the environment.

Dr. Mace used noise and slides in a room to assess responses among participants. Sounds were presented for 30 seconds along with a visual depiction for participants. These techniques were used for the Grand Canyon National Park and Hawaii parks. For the Grand Canyon, technicians used 40 and 80 dBA helicopter noise conditions; for Hawaii 40 and 60 dBA levels were used.

The findings suggested that visitors have different sensitivities in different soundscape settings. Helicopter noise was found to have a significant effect on evaluations of National Park soundscapes. All National Park vistas studied were found to have negative impacts with the presence of helicopter noise at 40, 60, and 80 dBA.

In another study, Dr. Mace tested to determine if subjects would moderate their feelings (annoyance, tranquility, etc.) based on the purpose of a helicopter flight in a National Park. In this study, it was found that there were no significant differences between the noise source conditions.

For a third set of studies, Dr. Mace and colleagues assessed visitor via surveys at lookouts (scenic vistas). The majority of visitors (55%) were bothered or annoyed by aircraft, and 25% of respondents believed that there were an excessive number of flights. Dr. Mace is conducting current soundscape research in Bryce Canyon that includes acoustic zones, attended listening, sound recording, visitor surveys, and lab-based assessments of different sounds for each acoustic zone.

For future research, it was suggested that specific dose-response relationships could be examined in the lab by expanding the response scales to include wilderness values. Lab research could be conducted to examine different management zones related to soundscapes. Using different acoustic zones within a park, visitors could be surveyed and attended logging data could be taken along with sound recordings. Lastly, observations methods could be used to track visitors at viewpoints in National Parks affected by aircraft overflights.

How can the value of the wilderness experience be defined and measured? (Presentation 1.5)
Bill Borrie

Bill Borrie conducted research for the US Department of Agriculture (USDA) and US Fish and Wildlife Service (FWS). From that work, Dr. Borrie has concluded a number of findings regarding surveys. Single item (i.e., noise) measures don't fare very well with surveys. Visitors and respondents don't have complete cognitive access to thoughts and feelings if they are measured off site – reliable recall may be beyond cognitive ability.

Participant responses become attuned to cultural norms instead of the environment context. Visitors possess selective attention to what they want to focus on. Visitors tend to blur over specific events and instead use "generic" evaluations. Often people will provide the most plausible answer. When visitors are asked to assess a past experience, mood becomes a proxy. Ordering the survey questions will also have an impact on the results. The more taxing the questions, the more participants will tailor their response.

Visitors have indicated high levels of satisfaction with their National Park visit in surveys. Visitor experiences are not necessarily goal directed or prescribed. Groups are more similar than different when describing their goals (e.g., wildlife viewing, natural scenery, learning opportunities, etc.).

The National Park managers are managing to create outstanding experiences. Measuring annoyance is not a helpful indicator for park managers. With the complexity of all the events associated with a park visit, it is difficult to process every occurrence. Within the framework of the Limits of Acceptable Change (LAC), management needs to identify the qualities to be preserved and the indicators of quality, and then to set the standards of acceptability.

 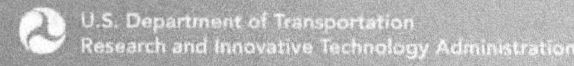

There is a need for an in-situ, multi-method approach for assessing exposure-response to noise. From a qualitative perspective, there is a need to assess how parks are perceived and experienced by visitors. Validation across different parks is useful so that qualities can be generalized. The public should be involved in the development of future standards.

6.3   Session 2

Data Gaps in Dose-Response Work (Presentation 2.1)
Nick Miller

Researchers have only completed aircraft dose-response work; there may be lessons to learn from conducting other types of noise measurements. Other sources of noise could include snow-machines, personal watercraft, high-altitude jets, and roadway traffic (varying noise over distance). Currently there is resistance to set a threshold because we don't know what the impacts will be on visitors or air tours.

Mr. Miller recommends that decision-makers physically participate in acoustic measurement activities or site visits. It is very informative to do an hour of logged listening. It may be possible to create an experience to evaluate at a number of sites.

Without these site visits, the decision makers will likely not understand the metrics and lack the ability to make sound policy. Only with the assistance of an acoustician can there be adequate identification of Soundscape resources. For example with air pollution – you can provide people with an assessment with parts per million data (pollutant concentrations in air), but unless you show them a photo (with the airborne pollution visible) they won't understand.

NPS has stated that the current assessment should not serve as the only metric. Using the analogy of air quality, a visitor may see the air quality as excellent, but it actually may be marginal from a planning perspective or historical conditions.

FAA stated that the agency is familiar with managing to protect resources, but not visitor preferences / experience. The agency believes strongly that whatever process is selected, it should be consistent from park to park.

Dose-Response Site selection based on Natural Soundscape Resource Protection (Presentation 2.2)
Dick Horonjeff

This presentation focused on the question, "Is visitor response to soundscape impairment more related to a non-auditory recreational activity, or a listening opportunity during the recreational activity?" Examples of listening opportunities include extreme quiet, animal calls and sounds, breeze in the trees, and moving water.

The premise offered is that multiple soundscapes may exist during the course of a single recreational visit. Two questions are linked to this premise: 1) Should different natural soundscapes be managed differently than other park material resources (e.g., ecological zones, geologic formations, etc.)?, and 2) If multiple natural soundscape opportunities exist, is it valuable to inventory them and adopt management policy to protect them?

The first step in this process would be to inventory the soundscape resources. This would involve identifying specific natural soundscape resources (opportunities) contained within a National Park. Next, potential impacts to the soundscape opportunities could be indentified. Then management could adopt actions to preserve the soundscape and maximize enjoyment.

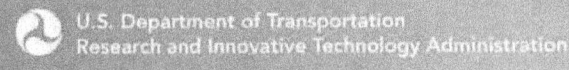
If this line of reasoning holds for listening opportunities, it would be useful to develop individual dose-response relationships for each type of soundscape. The soundscape factors might include measurement of opportunity-specific sensitivity, sporadic occurrences in duration in time or place (e.g., birdcalls), reaction to opportunity loss or impairment, and impairment type (e.g., air-tour helicopter, high altitude commercial flight).

One participant wondered if visitors to natural parks have the sophistication to make soundscape distinctions. The NPS stated that the approach described by Dr. Horonjeff is aligned with their goal to provide experiences of specific sound environments.

Major data gaps: How can they be resolved? (Presentation 2.3)
Grant Anderson

There is a major data gap with noise exposure-response work regarding backcountry visitors. Not only is it difficult to measure exposure due to the remoteness of the location, backcountry visitors will have different doses and responses over a multiple day/week periods. Visitors may have different responses during different activities. Backcountry visitors may experience a dose differently while hiking, preparing a meal, or relaxing at a campsite.

The challenges of backcountry visitor data are compounded by the following needs: location information in regular intervals, sufficiently precise dose exposure and measurements, and sufficiently thorough hiker survey responses.

For location, it may be possible to attach some sort of GPS monitor to a backpack. The unit could store months of discrete location data internally. Location data could be enhanced with a supplemental hiker log that would allow the visitor to record activities performed for each of the locations.

The responses could be recorded/surveyed at the end of each day and could include information on the when the visitor noticed aircraft. The survey could include a brief group of exposure questions. Visitors could compare doses to the previous day. Visitor would presumably know what the survey was measuring and this could negatively influence results. It would be helpful to reward the participants with some nominal cash or related reward for their efforts.

Sufficiently precise backcountry visitor doses may be difficult to obtain. One potential method is using the Air Traffic Control System Command Center. If this tool is used, study sites would be limited to areas with radar installations and relatively flat terrain. This information could be combined with RealContours to determine noise contours. A participant noted that this methodology would not be able to obtain relevant data to most National Parks as the FAA radar stations are not nearby.

An alternative method for recording backcountry doses could involve the use of a portable sound meter. Each unit could store about 100 days of storage in a single unit. The units need to be recharged after 24 hours of use adding a logistical challenge to this option.

Mr. Anderson proposed designing a program and implementing a study for 2-3 weeks at three National Parks. The dose-response backcountry visitor relationship and uncertainties could be determined from this study.

Alternative Exposure-Response Measurement Options (Presentation 2.4)
Amanda Rapoza

Researchers do not have data to develop exposure-response relationships for visitors in backcountry areas. Data gathering is logistically difficult due to the remote nature of the backcountry and the low visitation rates. Both these factors make it difficult to obtain and measure the visitor noise "dose" for such areas.

Certain characteristics of backcountry visitors may be found among visitors at other locations, however. It may be useful to establish exposure-response relationship among visitors at these locations as a proxy for backcountry exposure-response relationships. The level of attentiveness and individual expectations are two key attributes areas among backcountry to study for possible equivalent characteristics in less remote areas.

Attentiveness varies according to visitor activity, group size, presence of children within the visitor party, and crowding (density of other visitors). Attentiveness levels can be categorized in three general levels. Low attentiveness occurs when visitors are concentrating on a certain activity such as reading or conversing. A moderate level of attentiveness occurs when visitors are paying attention to their environment, but are simultaneously doing another activity like hiking or photography. High attentiveness occurs when a visitor is actively appreciating their surroundings such as viewing landscapes or actively listening. Higher attentiveness can be associated with very small visitor group size, no children present in group, no crowding conditions, and certain activities such as hiking, boating, and relaxing.

Expectations change according to the reason for the visit, previous trip experience(s), and knowledge of overflights. Backcountry visitors have a large range of prior visit experience and there is a large variation in the knowledge about overflights. The reason for backcountry visits often includes solitude as a central motivation.

It is likely that visitors could have similar levels of attentiveness in other non-backcountry locations; however, it is unlikely that similar expectations could be found. The data gathered at Bryce Canyon National Park is suggestive of a possible exposure-response relationship comparing visitors grouped into low and moderate levels of attentiveness.

If the backcountry visitor "proxy" approach is pursued further, it would be useful to develop a list of backcountry visitor characteristics, select the "key" characteristics from the list, and determine if these characteristics could be replicated at another location. Current data could be analyzed to assess if relationships are strengthened when these characteristics are included as factors. Researchers could identify surrogate sites with similar visitor characteristics and conduct a field test with large numbers of respondents. In addition, a limited amount of data from backcountry sites could be studied to see if the same trend is evident.

Site Selection and noise-exposure requirements for studying dose-response (Presentation 2.5)
Jim Fields

Before initiating new research, it is useful to review study priorities. Both the NPS and FAA have regulatory and management needs. New research should fulfill the following needs: 1) measurement of degree of impact on visitors, 2) measurement of impact for sensitive and mission-relevant activities, and 3) applications to all types of areas (scenic, historical, urban). Studies can be conducted on an activity basis (bird watching, interpretive talks, etc.), or location based (wilderness areas, overnight campsites, etc.).

Agencies should formulate strategy questions regarding mission sensitive activities. For example, does the most sensitive use dictate the policy even if there are other less sensitive uses nearby (i.e., short hikes adjacent to overlook sites)?

New studies should be conducted at sites with minimal noise data. Ambient noise should be considered in the study design as it varies greatly. The type of activity can also have a large impact.

NPS Regulations specify long-term site characteristics, not conditions for specific visits. The total impact on a visitor's complete resource experience (entire visit) cannot be determined from site experience measurement. The average impact at a site will be less than those that occur during the most sensitive conditions. It is difficult to predict the number of visits to an impacted site; visitation patterns are nonlinear and complex. The visitor demographic information may be irrelevant to routine NPS management practices (e.g., group size, and length of visit).

Sites differ in a large number of variables that necessitate data gathering at multiple sites to separate effects. There is bias from all the stakeholders (opinion survey, Acousticians, and Managers). There can be random and unanticipated differences between sites leading to overestimated precision in the results.

Studies should be designed with adequate variation within sites. The noise index variables are extremely important; yet only 2 of the sites with past noise dose-response studies have more than a 10-dB range in aircraft exposure. Ambient noise differences will also have large influence on the results. These challenges make it difficult to adopt management for sites with similar characteristics, when accuracy is better achieved for individual sites.

Researchers have learned some lessons from the past dose-response work. Site-visit data gathering is difficult. Of the 14 sites where data was collected, 3 were unusable for analysis, 4 others had fewer than 100 usable interviews, and 5 more had a narrow noise exposure band. Some visitors left the interview areas before they could be approached by staff. Of the 2,785 interviews conducted about 25 percent were unusable.

For future research, Dr. Fields provided a number of suggestions before any additional data gathering is pursued:
- Assess the potential site visit / site management mismatch using current site-visit findings.
- Perform an analysis of all existing US data with full stakeholder involvement (NPS, FAA) and utilize a range of consultants.
- Set precise statistical requirements for future studies with NPS and FAA working with consultants
- Develop a survey design evaluation tool to estimate the likely precision of estimates from any proposed study design.
- Gather information on potential sites that would provide the strongest design conditions.
- Evaluate alternative designs and research projects using statistical design tools.
- Choose projects or revise policy goals/study plans/assumptions to form new study designs.

6.4   Summary of Discussions

General Discussion and summary of key ideas from Session 1

As a starting point, participants recommended a comprehensive review of noise dose-response work to mine existing data and to incorporate research from both disciplines (engineering and sociology). According to participants, the researchers should be able to determine the potential for new findings quickly. The existing data were measured according to strict parameters detailed by NPS, making replication of methodology possible. Researchers did not record all of the site characteristics at the 14 sites so generalizations about NPS management zones may not be possible.

Participants also expressed the need for a more systematic approach in future research efforts. The systematic approach would ideally combine engineering and sociological research methods and involve regular consultation with Federal agencies. Additionally, data gathering opportunities could be maximized with engineers and sociologists gathering data simultaneously. This comprehensive effort could better utilize multiple research methods, identify data gaps, and determine indicators and standards for measurement. NPS, FAA and academic researchers will keep the group informed of future plans and help to identify opportunities for cooperative research.

All the groups identified a need for a white paper to establish a new research framework. The white paper could be jointly authored by engineer(s) and sociologist(s), and could create a system to generalize conditions across National Park management zones. In addition, the white paper could evaluate all prior studies related to visitor dose-response. Coordinated research offers greater benefits than a continuation

of disconnected piecemeal studies. Ideally, the quantitative research and the qualitative research can inform each other.

The groups also recommended explicit Federal guidance in a number of areas. Researchers stated that it will ultimately be up to parties at the NPS and FAA to determine acceptable noise thresholds, science can only inform this decision. If the current group of active NPS and FAA stakeholders are unable to reach agreement on thresholds, the issue should be elevated to the appropriate authority to make final determinations.

The decentralized decision-making process at individual parks combined with the huge variation across National Park units makes it challenging to adopt general guidelines regarding noise impacts on visitors. Nevertheless, researchers emphasized the benefits of pre-determined National Park management goals related to park resource/management areas.

NPS representatives at the workshop stated that park managers seek to optimize visitors' total experience. The preference of NPS is finding methods to preserve the natural environment and measuring "annoyance" levels may offer little value to the park managers. Researchers could focus on selecting soundscape "indicators," determining reasonable flight restrictions such as flight-free zones and seasonal/temporal restrictions, and establishing "noise-free" intervals. Any interference with the "natural quiet" is viewed as a key impact.

Workshop participants suggested a review of research findings related to the concept of "solitude" for an analogy on what the research progression might be for "natural quiet" and noise impacts on visitors. Due to the complexity of backcountry research and multiple interpretations of solitude, it has been difficult to both measure impacts on solitude and define the concept. After a body of research is compiled and sufficient dialogue among technical experts, a consensus might be reached regarding impacts on solitude (e.g., more than 3-5 encounters with other backcountry visitors degrades a solitude experience).

Dose-response work in relation to ongoing NEPA work

The FAA and NPS agreed that it is too late into the NEPA process to incorporate any new dose-response work into the Mount Rushmore environmental document. It may be possible to incorporate recent studies gathered by Steve Lawson into the Hawaii parks NEPA work. It is unlikely either the Grand Canyon or the Hawaii parks could use any new studies that may be generated as a result of this workshop. The agencies agreed that expert input and review would be helpful to test hypotheses for future work.

It is should be noted that the Office of Management and Budget (OMB) review of surveys and information collection requirements require about 18 months of lead time before any new survey data can be collected from the public. It would be beneficial to begin the information collection background work as soon as possible to minimize the delays associated with the OMB process.

7.0   Next Steps

Three primary actions were suggested to advance noise exposure / human response research:
- Further analysis of existing data. All participants agreed that existing data should be reassessed to maximize the use of already conducted measurements and to help steer the direction of future measurements.

- Development of a white paper. A white paper would summarize the existing data, identify the data gaps, provide suggestions for combining quantitative and qualitative research, and create a framework for future research that would generalize conditions across National Park management zones.

- Convene a future meeting of technical experts. It was agreed that a follow up meeting would be necessary to discuss determine the best way to proceed for future research. The meeting would be expected to require two to three days of discussion. At the meeting, technical experts could: 1) Identify all the barriers to determining adverse noise impacts on the visitor experience, 2) make recommendations to address the barriers, 3) determine an acceptable range of NPS land-uses and certain parcels as homogenous for land management considerations, 4) identify types of NPS visitors and associated expectations, and 5) list acoustic/listening opportunities. The technical experts requested funding to cover related expenses including an estimated 2 to 3 days of workshop attendance, 2 days of preparation and 2 days of travel.

  Before this meeting, both the FAA and NPS will provide workshop participants with additional technical distinctions that will assist with resource assessments. The FAA will provide follow up information regarding airspace management considerations and types of aircraft. In addition, the FAA will supply data on the different types of operators and proximity of air force bases. The NPS will share information to create a resource "matrix" covering management zones, types of visitors, impacts, and contexts.

NPS and FAA have discussed how they can fund this process. Both agencies have committed to making the research possible. A separate meeting with only Federal representatives was conducted during the workshop to discuss acquisition strategies.

Appendix A – Presentation Slides

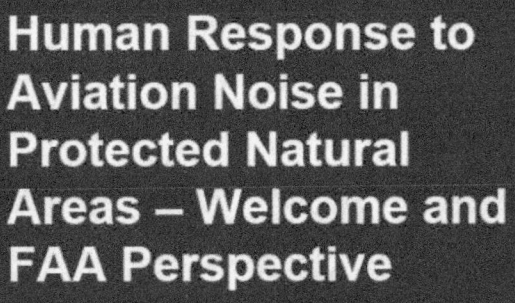

Human Response to Aviation Noise in Protected Natural Areas – Welcome and FAA Perspective

Federal Aviation Administration

Presented at: Exposure-Response Workshop

By: Barry Brayer, Manager, AWP-1SP

Date: October 28, 2008

Opening Remarks

- **Welcome Your Expertise to this Timely Workshop**

- **Your Participation is Important**

- **Help us to build the framework leading to reasonable scientific methods for analyzing aircraft impacts at national parks**

Exposure-Response Workshop
October 28-29, 2008

Federal Aviation
Administration

2

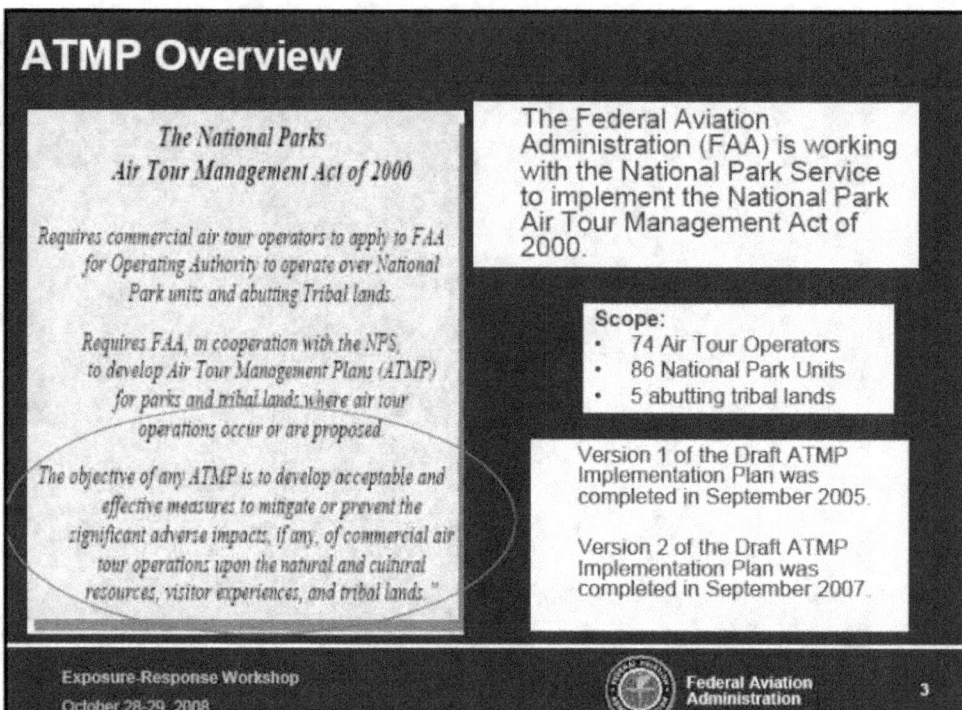

ATMP Overview

The National Parks
Air Tour Management Act of 2000

Requires commercial air tour operators to apply to FAA for Operating Authority to operate over National Park units and abutting Tribal lands.

Requires FAA, in cooperation with the NPS, to develop Air Tour Management Plans (ATMP) for parks and tribal lands where air tour operations occur or are proposed.

The objective of any ATMP is to develop acceptable and effective measures to mitigate or prevent the significant adverse impacts, if any, of commercial air tour operations upon the natural and cultural resources, visitor experiences, and tribal lands."

The Federal Aviation Administration (FAA) is working with the National Park Service to implement the National Park Air Tour Management Act of 2000.

Scope:
- 74 Air Tour Operators
- 86 National Park Units
- 5 abutting tribal lands

Version 1 of the Draft ATMP Implementation Plan was completed in September 2005.

Version 2 of the Draft ATMP Implementation Plan was completed in September 2007.

Exposure-Response Workshop
October 28-29, 2008

Federal Aviation Administration

3

National Parks and Air Tour Noise

- FAA Special Programs Office, is the nationwide lead for the Air Tour Management Plan (ATMP) program and also provides support on the Grand Canyon Overflights Environmental Impact Statement (EIS)
- The ATMP program and the Grand Canyon Overflights project require the FAA to work in cooperation with the National Park Service (NPS) in developing the required environmental documentation
- Currently preparing environmental documents for ATMPs at Mount Rushmore and Badlands National Parks in South Dakota and Haleakala and Hawaii Volcanoes National Parks in Hawaii, as well as EIS for Grand Canyon Overflights project.
- For ATMPs, agencies have differing views on which noise metrics and reference ambient data to use, as well as different impact determinations
- A Technical Team has been set up to vet the metrics and analysis to be used in support of the Grand Canyon Overflights EIS

Exposure-Response Workshop
October 28-29, 2008

Federal Aviation Administration

4

National Parks and Air Tour Noise

- Agencies realize that there are data gaps in our knowledge to be able to address noise impacts in naturally quiet areas
- One of the main challenges is to develop a technically defensible approach for determining significant noise impacts from aviation-related projects in naturally quiet areas
- Special Programs Office is currently funding a number of research projects through Volpe, with FAA's Office of Environment and Energy as technical lead, to meet this goal
- Noise exposure-response relationships and thresholds were identified as highest value research project to support our ATMP program
- Looking for your assistance in identifying / prioritizing research projects that will fill in these gaps and assist us in our environmental impact analysis

Exposure-Response Workshop
October 28-29, 2008

 Federal Aviation Administration

5

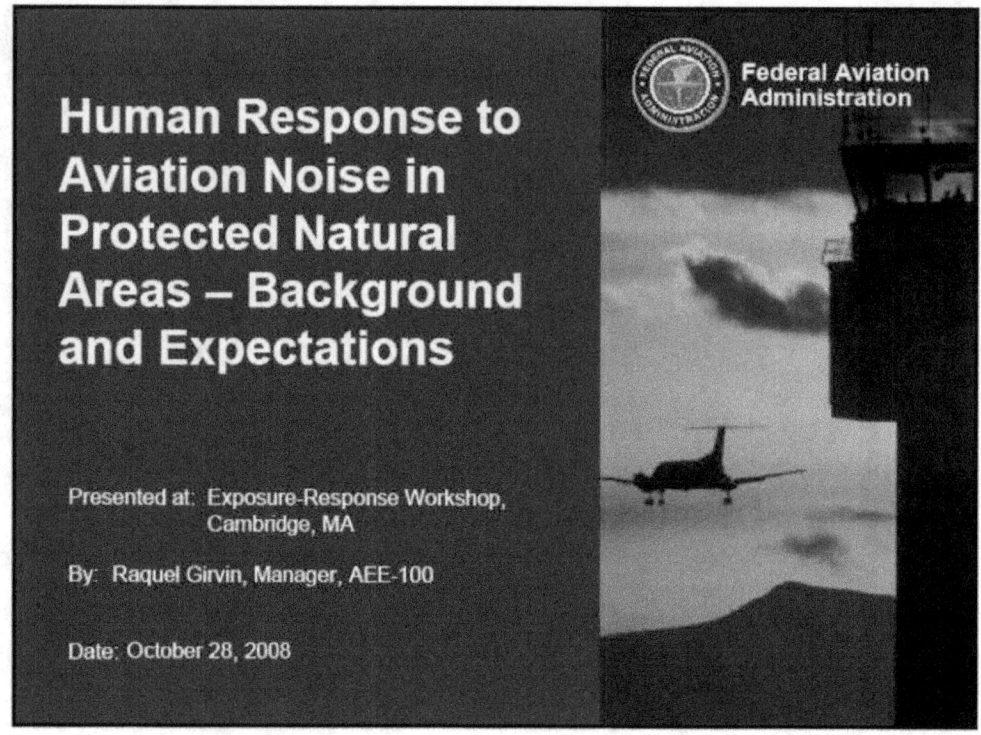

Drivers for this Workshop

- Noise impact analyses needed as part of National Parks Air Tour Management Plans (ATMP)

- National Parks Air Tour Management Act of 2000 states that any methodology adopted by a Federal agency to assess air tour noise under this Act shall be based on reasonable scientific methods (Sec. 808)

- Noise impact analyses at National Parks also needed to comply with NEPA for airport and airspace redesign projects

Exposure-Response Workshop
October 28-29, 2008

 Federal Aviation Administration

2

Noise Impact Analysis – Background

- FAA Order 1050.1E

  Environmental Impacts: Policies and Procedures

  – "An EIS…provides…a full and fair discussion of significant environmental impacts of the proposed action and reasonable alternatives…" [Ch. 5 Section 500a.(1)]

  – "An EIS shall be prepared for major Federal actions significantly affecting the quality of the human environment… Significance is defined in terms of context and intensity…" [Ch. 5 Section 501.]

  – "Significance varies with the setting of the proposed action… Both short- and long-term effects are relevant." [Ch. 5 Section 501a.]

Exposure-Response Workshop
October 28-29, 2008

 Federal Aviation Administration

3

Noise Impact Analysis for ATMP – Background

- Scope

  – Agencies have agreed to expand noise impact analysis within a National Park's boundaries to include impacts to the park's *natural soundscape*

  – Outside National Parks' boundaries, ATMP noise impact analysis will follow standard policies and procedures outlined in FAA Order 1050.1E

Exposure-Response Workshop
October 28-29, 2008

 Federal Aviation Administration

4

Noise Impact Analysis for ATMP – Background

- The challenge
  - How to analyze noise impacts to visitors of National Parks:
    - FAA recognizes that the 65 DNL significant noise threshold inadequately addresses effects of noise on visitors in naturally quiet areas such as National Parks
    - While noise in excess of 65 DNL within a park will be considered significant, the significance of impacts in excess of NPS "minor" impact descriptors but less than 65 DNL remains to be determined
    - Need to account for many variables that impact visitor experience

Exposure-Response Workshop
October 28-29, 2008

 Federal Aviation Administration

5

Noise Impact Analysis for ATMP – Background

- An approach
  - Visitor exposure-response relationships offer a potential basis for establishing metrics and thresholds to analyze noise impacts in National Parks
    - Surveying visitors and acquiring noise data should help us understand how noise affects the "quality of the human environment" in terms of what bothers people
    - But deriving noise exposure-response relationships for National Parks visitors - that are scientifically defensible and sufficiently generalizable - remains elusive

Exposure-Response Workshop
October 28-29, 2008

 Federal Aviation Administration

6

Goal and Objective of this Workshop

Goal
- To establish a scientifically defensible approach for measuring and modeling the characteristics of noise exposure that correlate with visitors' evaluation of how noise affects the quality of their environment in different National Parks

Main Objective
- To develop roadmap that will advance research and produce a reliable body of data on National Parks visitors' response to aircraft noise exposure

Exposure-Response Workshop
October 28-29, 2008

 Federal Aviation Administration

7

What we expect to accomplish at this Workshop

- **Establish common understanding of findings from exposure-response research and data analysis completed to date since this will be our starting point**
  - Weaknesses/strengths
  - Lessons learned: methodology, gaps, etc.
  - What, if any, questions has research answered regarding noise impacts to National Park visitors
  - What else might be gleaned from available data

Exposure-Response Workshop
October 28-29, 2008

 Federal Aviation Administration

8

What we expect to accomplish at this Workshop

- **Prioritize key questions that must be answered by follow-on research**
- **Propose and discuss multiple potential paths to answer key questions**
- **"Downselect" to a research roadmap**

Exposure-Response Workshop
October 28-29, 2008

 Federal Aviation Administration

9

Questions to be answered

In developing the research roadmap, consider:
- How can we improve measurement of visitor response?
- How many and what response variables are needed to adequately span the range of desired visitor experiences (annoyance, interference with enjoyment, appropriateness, …)?
- What sound measurements and noise exposure metrics merit exploration as predictors of survey responses?
- Can we compute these metrics and validate how we compute them?
- What factors need to be controlled to improve the capacity of models to predict responses to noise?
- Is visitor response different for infrequent but louder aircraft noise versus more frequent but quieter aircraft noise?
- What non-acoustic factors may affect visitor response?
- For pooled models that span multiple parks, what generic characteristics should be examined to explain variation in responses across sites and parks?

Ultimately, questions we'll need to answer:
- Which noise metric or combination of metrics should we use to predict visitor response to aircraft noise in naturally quiet areas?
- Based on these identified metric(s), what threshold(s) represent(s) significance?
- What mitigation measures would be considered beneficial in reducing human response impacts from aircraft noise?

Exposure-Response Workshop
October 28-29, 2008

 Federal Aviation Administration

10

Concluding remarks

- **Progress in completing ATMPs for 86 park units depends on research as ATMP development is ongoing**
- **Research alignment is critical as much time has elapsed with limited progress**
- **This is our opportunity to work together towards a common goal**
  - Pursue open and constructive dialogue
  - Seek practicable approaches
  - Maintain focus on objective

Exposure-Response Workshop
October 28-29, 2008

 Federal Aviation Administration

11

Thank you for agreeing to participate

Exposure-Response Workshop
October 28-29, 2008

 Federal Aviation Administration

12

www.hmmh.com

Development
of
Visitor Dose-Response Relationships

Nicholas P. Miller

Harris Miller Miller & Hanson Inc.

National Parks and Visitor Response to Sounds
Outline

www.hmmh.com

- **Park Acoustic Environments**
- **Dose-Response Method**
  - Data Collection
  - Data Analysis
- **Results**
  - Short Hike v. Overlook sites
  - Annoyance and Interference
  - Effect of Expectations

National Parks and Visitor Response to Sounds
Park Acoustic Environments

www.hmmh.com

- A "Different" Sound Environment
  - Can be Extremely Quiet
  - Standard Noise Metrics May Not Apply
  - Standard Assessment Methods May Not Apply

National Parks and Visitor Response to Sounds
Park Acoustic Environments

www.hmmh.com

A-Weighted Sound Level (decibels)	Typical Outdoor Setting	
80		
	Noisy Urban (daytime)	
70		
	Commercial Retail Area	**Non-Park**
60		
	Suburban (daytime)	
50		
	Suburban (nighttime)	
40		
	Grand Canyon (along river)	
30		
	Hawaii Volcanoes (crater overlook)	
20		**Park**
	Grand Canyon (remote trail)	
10		
	Haleakala (in crater, no wind)	
0		

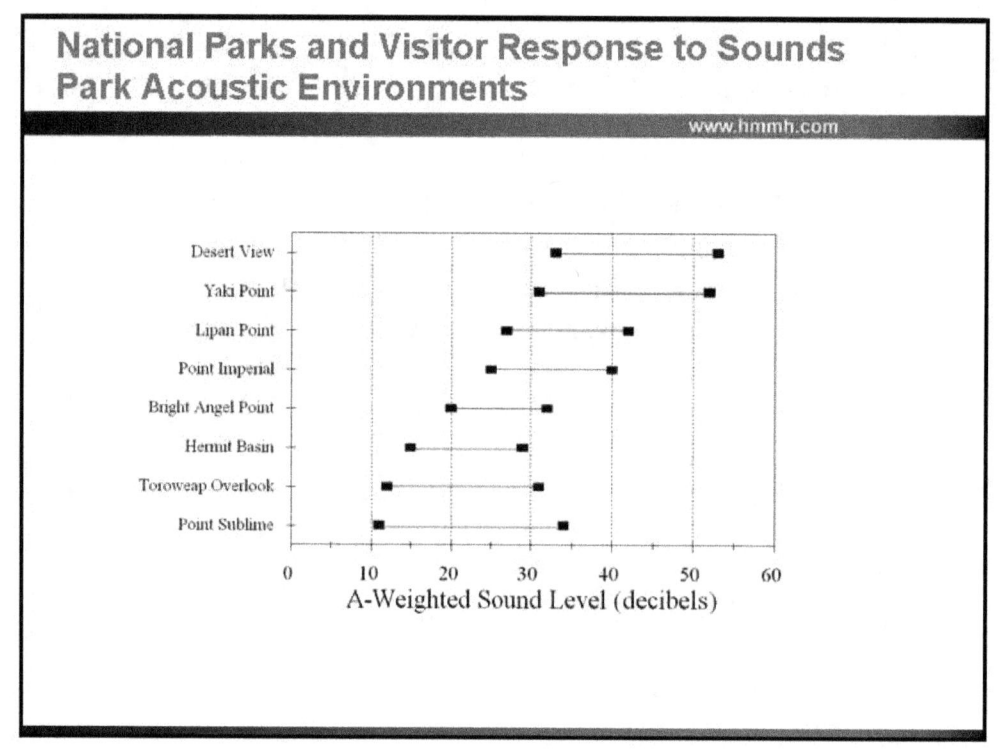

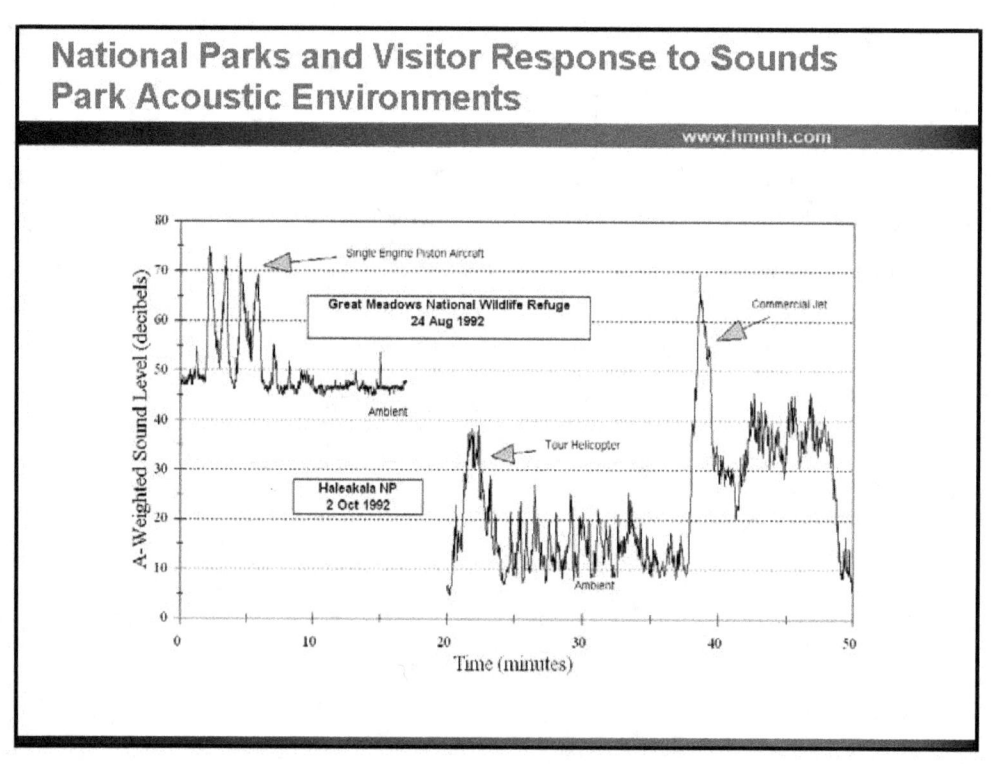

National Parks and Visitor Response to Sounds
Dose-Response Method - Doses

www.hmmh.com

- **What doses should we / can we determine?**
  - Quiet may mean special "low noise" equipment
  - Standard metrics
    - Maximum levels
    - Equivalent levels
    - Sound Exposure Level
  - Need to separate "natural" from "non-natural"
  - Could not accomplish with equipment only

- **Concluded:**
  - One-second A-weighted levels (only reasonably available)
  - "Observer Logging" – second by second identification

National Parks and Visitor Response to Sounds
Dose-Response Method - Responses

www.hmmh.com

- **Visitor Responses**
  - Annoyance standard – NPS used moderately, very and extremely (not standard two top out of five)
  - Interference with:
    - Enjoyment
    - Natural quiet and sounds of nature
    - Appreciation of historical / cultural significance
  - Acceptability of:
    - Number of aircraft
    - Level of sound
    - Time heard

- **Developed 5 – 7 Minute Questionnaire**

National Parks and Visitor Response to Sounds
Dose-Response Method – Mediators

www.hmmh.com

- Mediators
  - Size of group
  - Gender
  - Age
  - Prior visits
  - Type of site
  - Presence of children in group
  - Type of aircraft

National Parks and Visitor Response to Sounds
Dose-Response Method – Data Collection

www.hmmh.com

- **Selection of Data Collection Sites**
  - Visitation Rate - 5 to 10 groups / hour
  - Number of Overflights - minimum 2 to 4 / hour
  - Size of Area - Characterize w/ single monitor
  - Ease of Interviewing - Single entry / exit point
  - Visit Duration - minimum 15 minutes
  - Few Additional Noise Sources
  - All Visitor Activity Outdoors

National Parks and Visitor Response to Sounds
Dose-Response Method – Data Collection

www.hmmh.com

Park	Study Area	Type Area	Number of Respondents	Range of Typical Background Leq, dB(A)	Aircraft per Hour (approx.)
Grand Canyon	Lipan Point	Overlook	193	40-50	24
	Point Imperial	Overlook	124	25-40	22
	Havasu Creek	Short Hike	30	65-70	9
	Hermit Basin	Short Hike	32	20-25	31
Haleakala	Sliding Sands	Short Hike	213	20-30	8
Hawaii Volcanos	Wahaula	Short Hike	180	35-45	9

National Parks and Visitor Response to Sounds
Dose-Response Method – Data Collection

www.hmmh.com

National Parks and Visitor Response to Sounds
Dose-Response Method – Analysis

www.hmmh.com

- **At a Specific Park Location Simultaneously:**
  - Measure Sound Levels
  - Identify all Sources of Sound (second-by-second observer)
  - Interview Visitors on Exiting Area
- **Combine / Analyze the Three Data Sets**
- **Perform Logistic Regression**
  - Explore Several Dose-Response Combinations
  - Examine Effects of Mediators

National Parks and Visitor Response to Sounds
Dose-Response Method – Results

www.hmmh.com

ANNOYANCE (MODERATE TO EXTREME) versus PERCENTAGE OF TIME THAT AIRCRAFT CAN BE HEARD

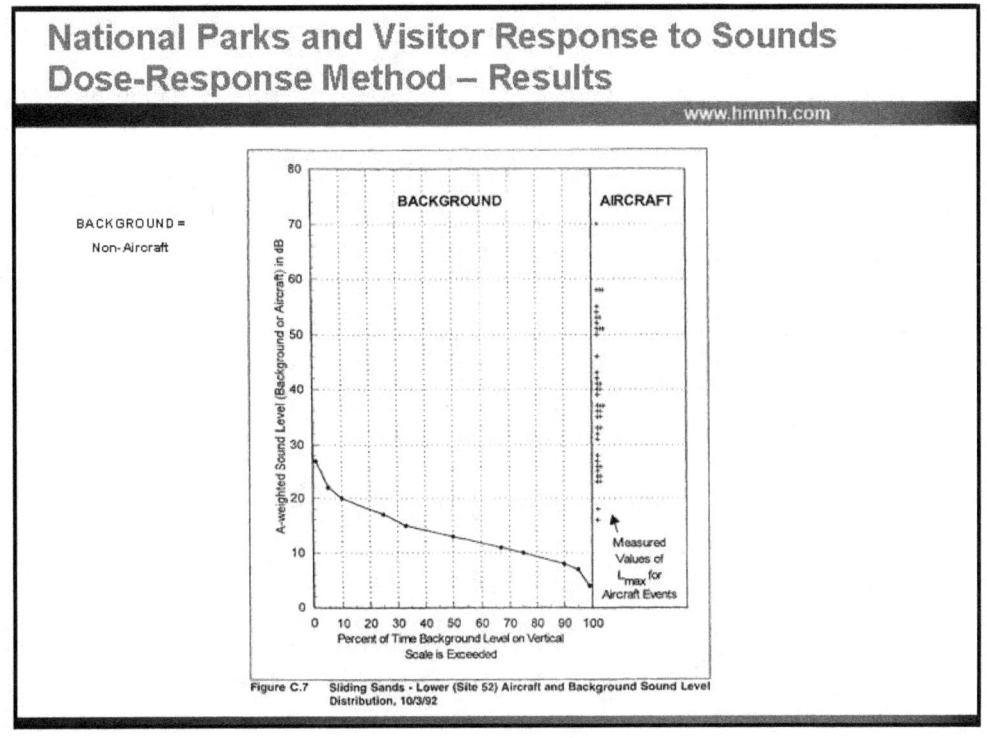

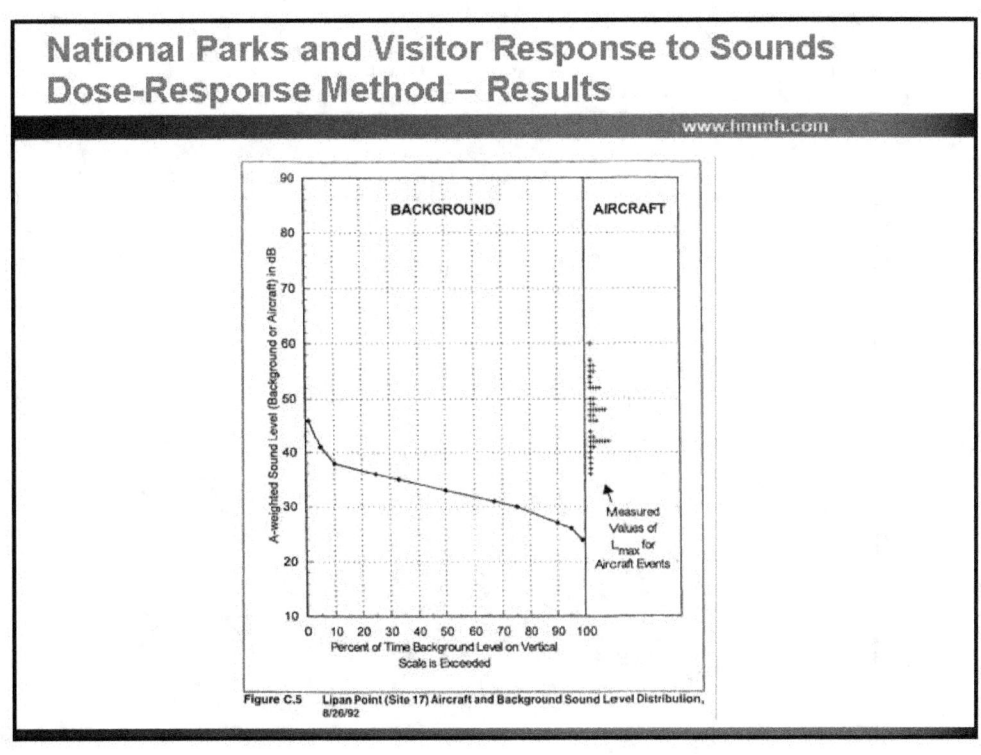

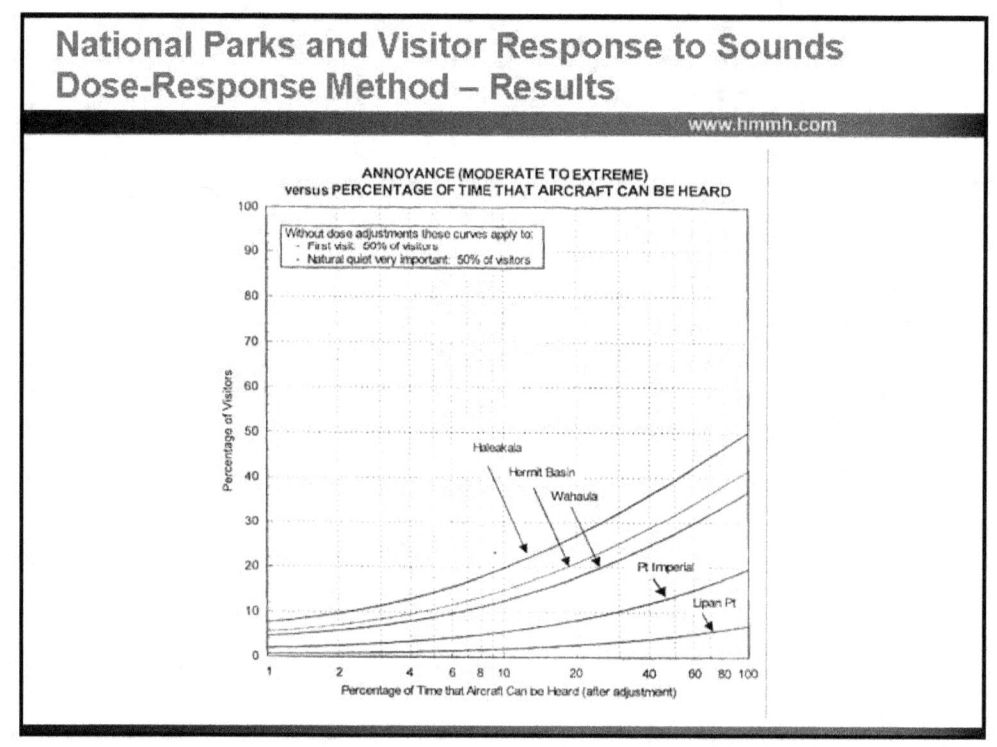

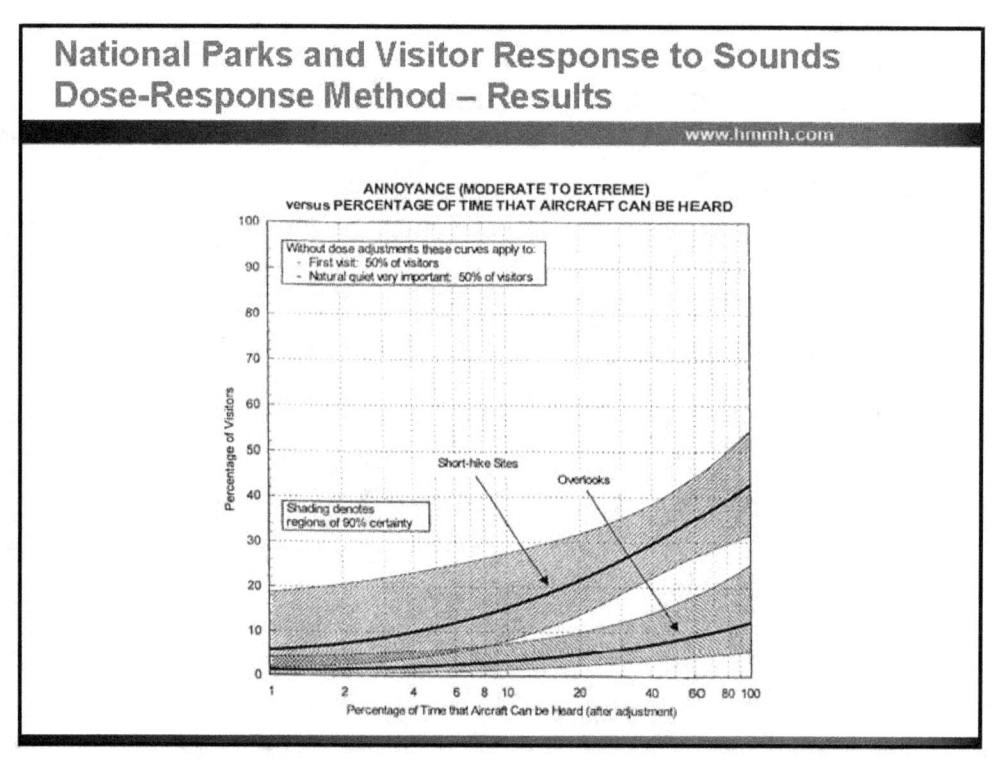

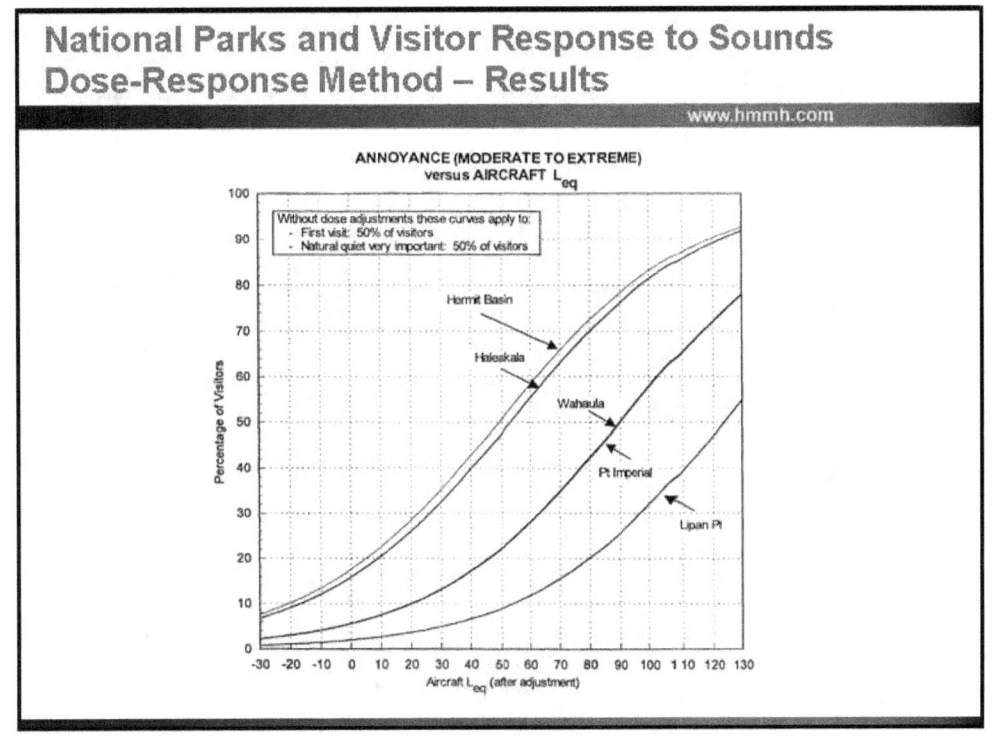

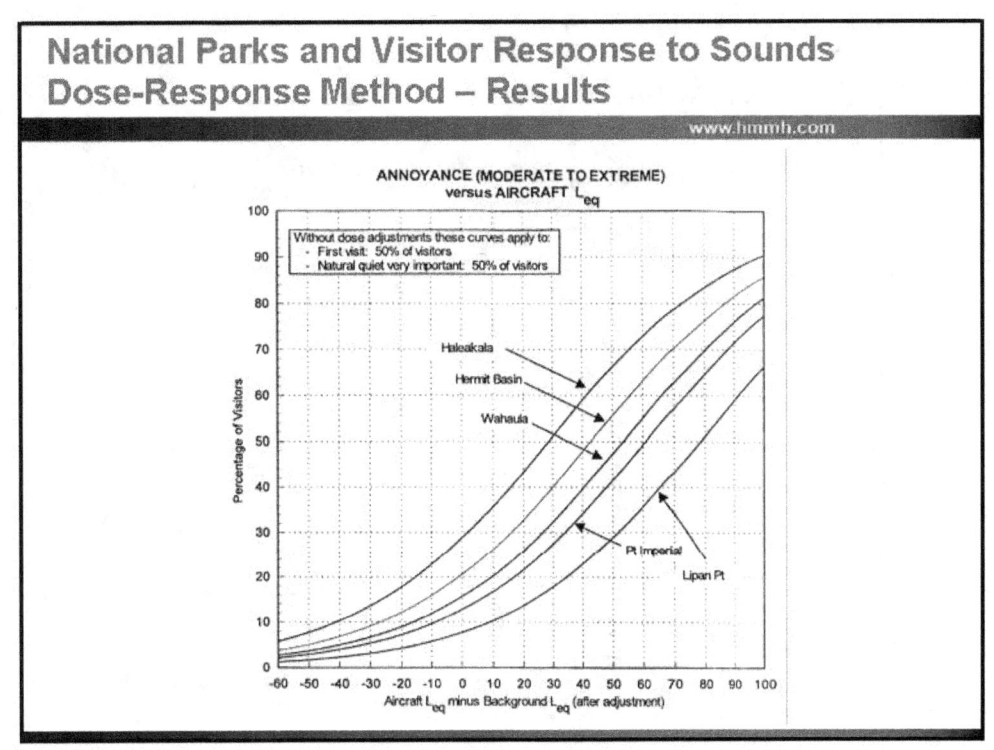

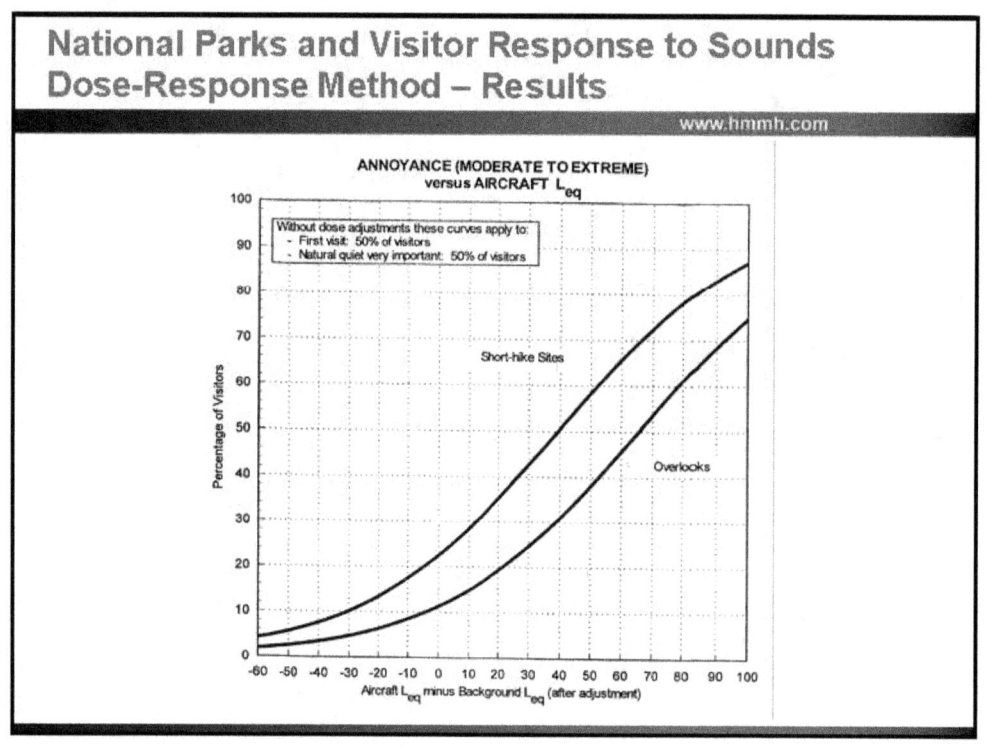

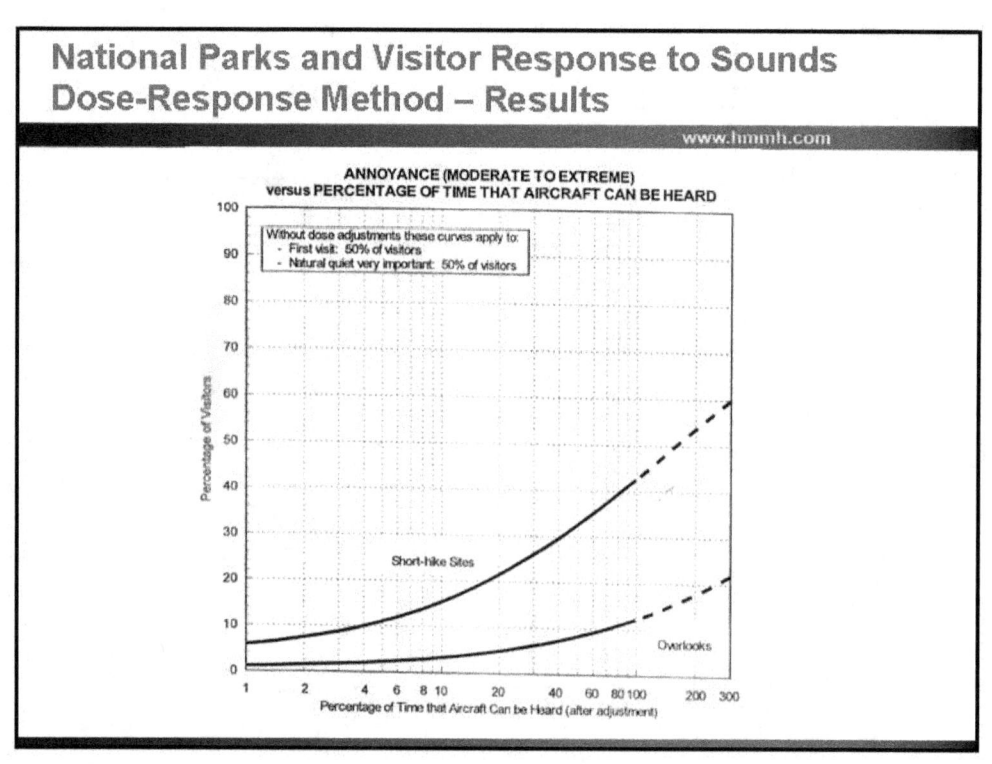

National Parks and Visitor Response to Sounds
Dose-Response Method – Results

www.hmmh.com

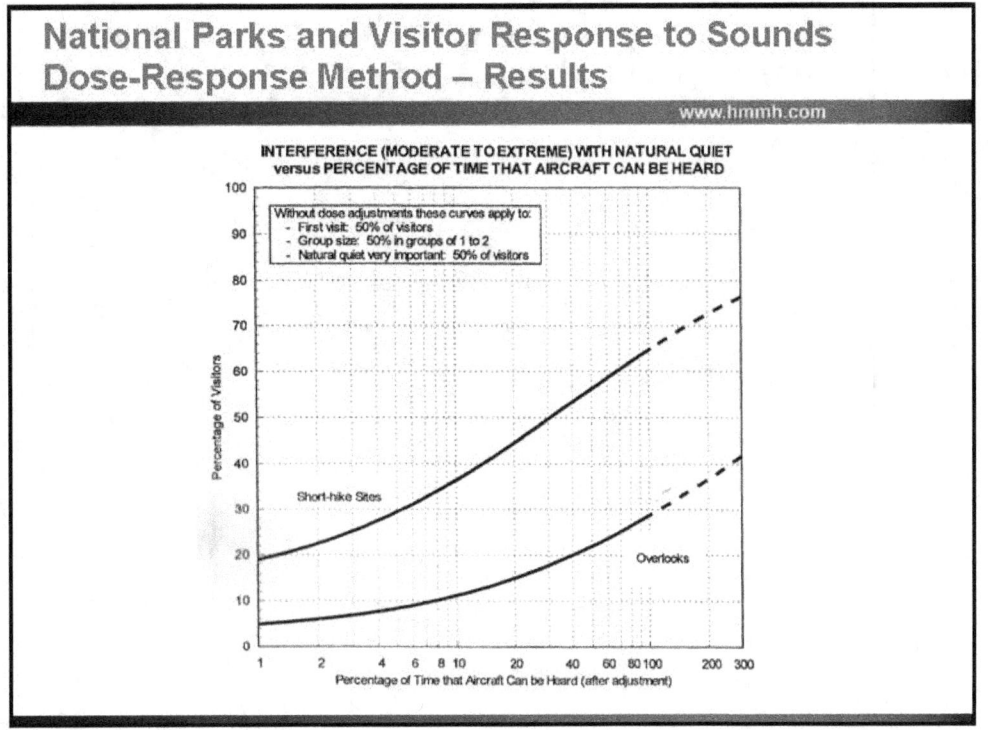

National Parks and Visitor Response to Sounds
Dose-Response Method – Results

www.hmmh.com

- **At White Sands National Monument**
  - Tested effect of knowledge
  - Placed sign at trail head for ~ 50% of time

"MILITARY AIRCRAFT CAN REGULARLY BE SEEN AND HEARD ON THIS WALK"

National Parks and Visitor Response to Sounds
Dose-Response Method – Results

www.hmmh.com

Remembered Information	Sign Up		Sign Down	
	Number	Percent	Number	Percent
Sign	69	40%	0	0%
Other Information	41	24%	50	28%
None	63	36%	126	63%
TOTAL	173	100%	176	100%

National Parks and Visitor Response to Sounds
Dose-Response Method – Results

www.hmmh.com

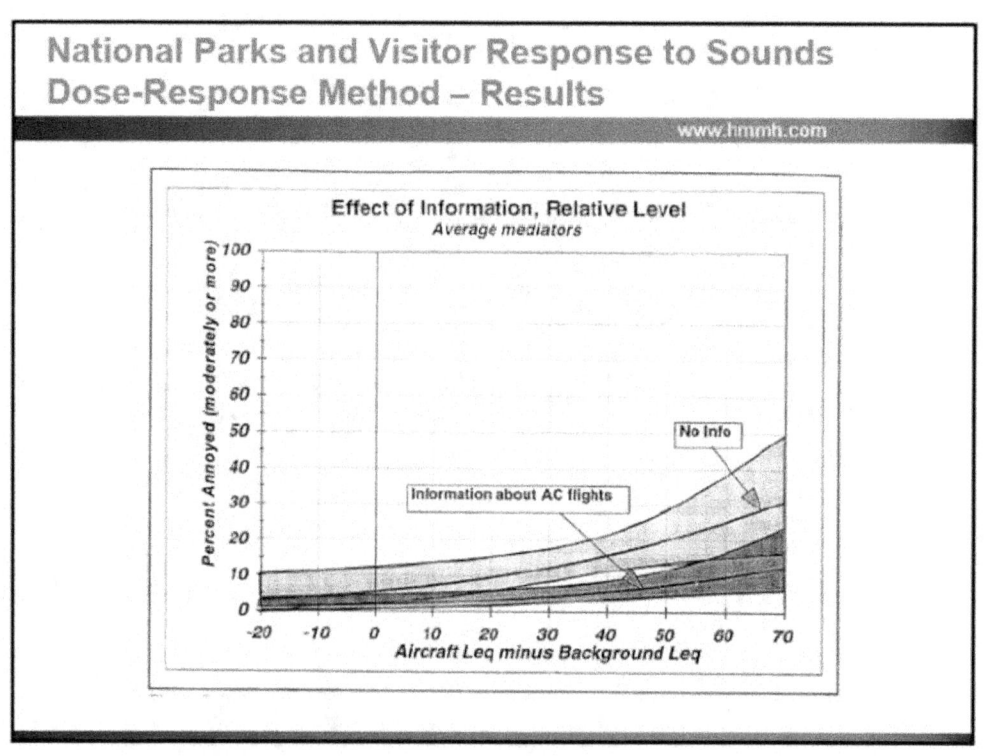

42

**National Parks and Visitor Response to Sounds
Dose-Response Method – Results**

www.hmmh.com

- Visitor sensitivity varies site-to-site
- First time visitors less sensitive
- Visit to enjoy natural quiet more sensitive
- Groups of >2 people less sensitive
- More report interference w/ NQ than report annoyance
- Interference and annoyance distinctly different
- Grouping of aircraft seems to reduce annoyance
- Knowing about aircraft reduces annoyance

**National Parks and Visitor Response to Sounds
Dose-Response Method – Reports**

www.hmmh.com

- Anderson, G.S., et al, "Dose-Response Relationships Derived from Data Collected at Grand Canyon, Haleakala and Hawaii Volcanoes National Park," HMMH Report No. 290940.14, NPOA Report 93-6, October 1993
  - First field study of acoustic dose-response in park setting
  - Developed methods – instrumentation, interviewing, observer logging
  - Sound measurements, observations, doses on one-second basis
  - Five sites
- Miller, N.P., et al, "Mitigating the Effects of Military Aircraft Overflights on Recreational Users of Parks," USAF Report AFRL-HE-WP-TR-2000-0034, July 1999
  - Further refinement – one site, larger sample size
  - Explored expectations / prior knowledge of sounds

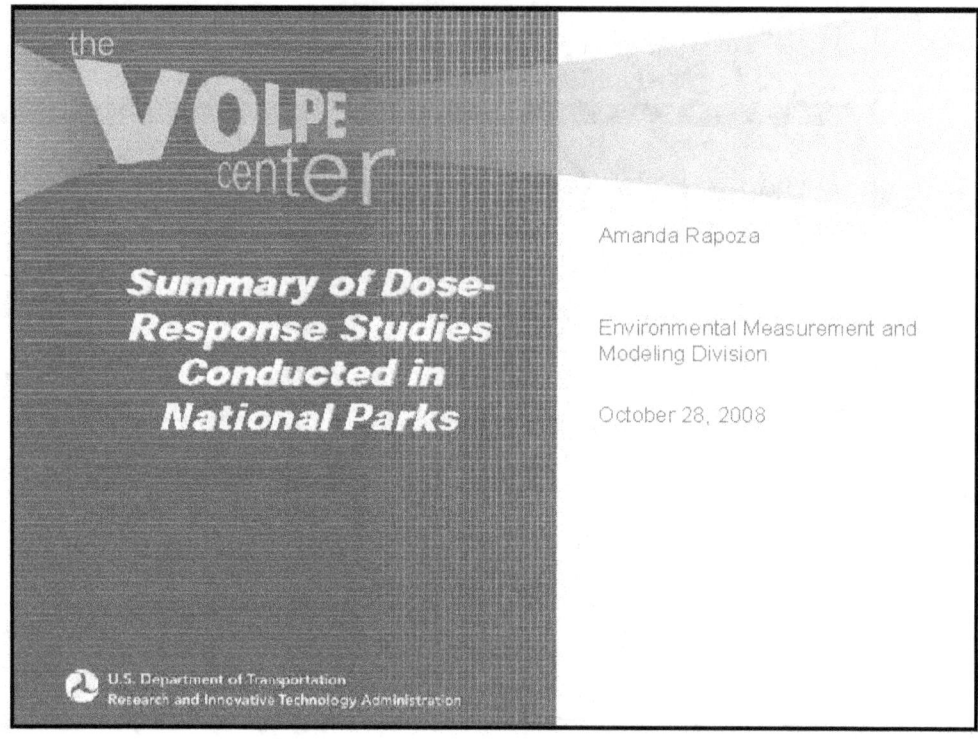

1997 Bryce Canyon Study

- Expanded the short hike dose-response database.
  - → 905 'good' data points for 1 trail
- Examined the predictive power of additional acoustic dose descriptors. (%TN, %TAA, ΔL_{AE} Which performs best for this dataset?)
  1. $\Delta L_{AE,}$ %TA, %Ta$_{w/ojet}$
- Examined mediating factors which could be included in a National Rule
  1. Gender, group size, presence of children significant
- Examined alternate statistical analysis methods to improve predictive power of dose-response relationships.

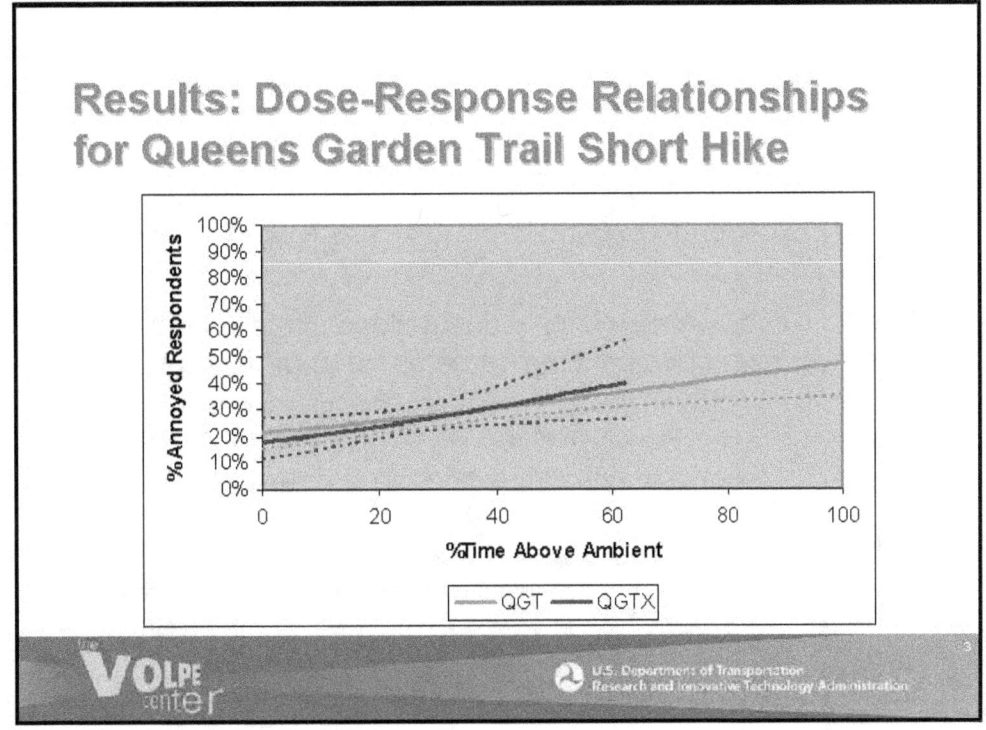

Results: Dose-Response Relationships for Queens Garden Trail Short Hike

---

1997 Bryce Canyon Study

Strengths:

- Wide variation in of sound level and time above
- 905 data points at one site

Criticisms:

- Relationships based on annoyance response.
- Desire for simplicity – mediators were not included in final model.
- Only one site – can these relationships be used to define impacts at other sites & parks?

1998 Bryce Canyon/Grand Canyon Overlook Study

Follow-on to expand overlook dose-response database

- Determine which acoustic descriptors predict well at overlooks (Is it the same as for short hikes?)
  - → %Time Above Ambient was the only acoustic descriptor which performed well at both short hikes and overlooks.
- Confirm that visitor response is different between short hikes and overlooks at Bryce Canyon.
  - → In instances of equal noise dose, visitors at short hike sites will be more annoyed than visitors at overlook sites.

VOLPE center
U.S. Department of Transportation
Research and Innovative Technology Administration

1998 Bryce Canyon/Grand Canyon Overlook Study

- **Collect additional data at Point Imperial – does the relationship change over time?**
  - → There appears to be no change in visitor response over time

VOLPE center
U.S. Department of Transportation
Research and Innovative Technology Administration

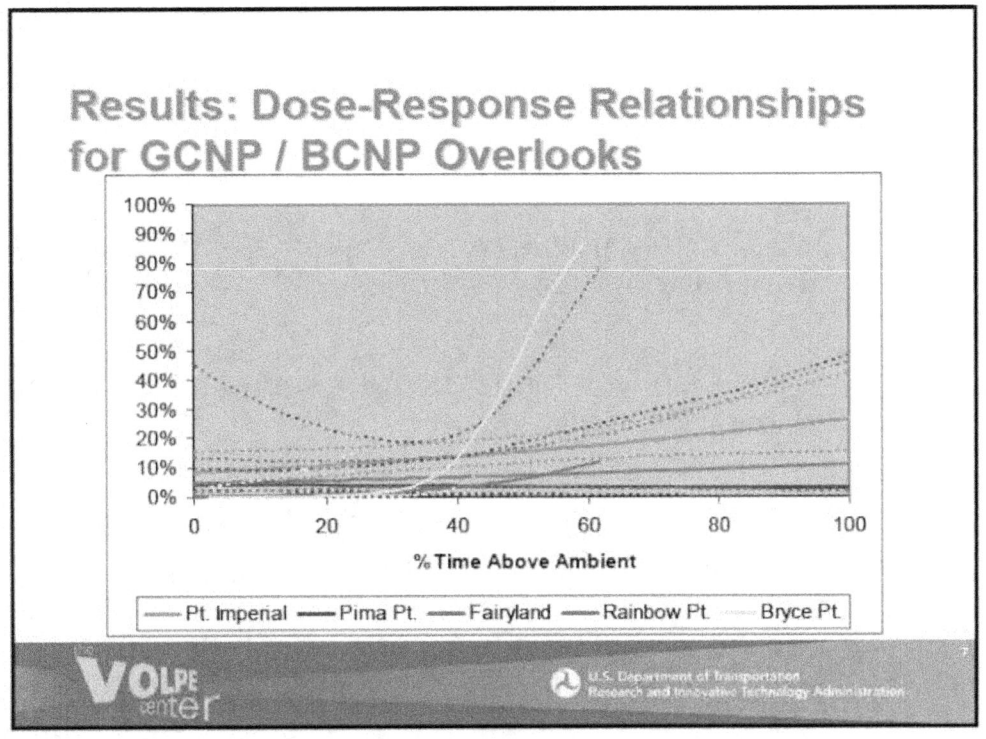

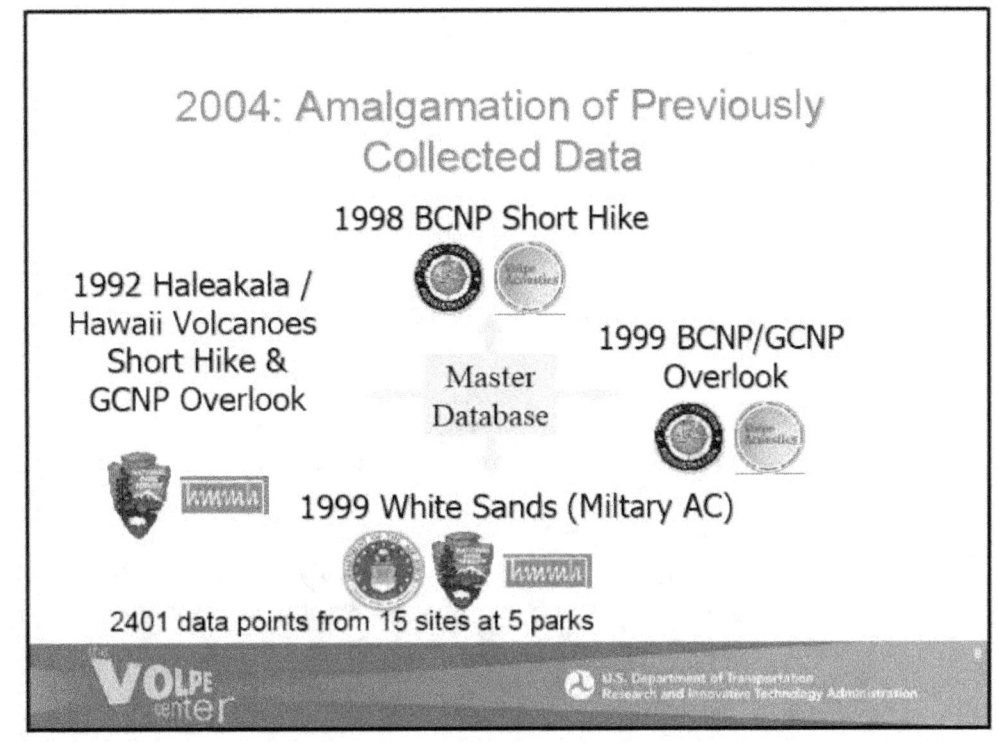

2004: Amalgamation of Previously Collected Data

✓ 2303 data points from 14 sites at 4 parks (Data from military AC were not used)

✓ Develop 'combined' dose-response relationships.

✓ Compare relationships to answer key questions regarding the behavior of visitor response.

VOLPE center

U.S. Department of Transportation
Research and Innovative Technology Administration

9

What is the best way to characterize noise exposure?

✓ %TA
✓ TAA
✓ %TAA**
✓ $L_{Aeq,1h}$

✓ $L_{Aeq,Tresp}$
✓ $\Delta L_{AE,Tac}$
✓ $\Delta L_{AE,Tresp}$
✓ NUM_{ac}

✗ %TN
✗ $L_{Aeq,Tac}$
✗ L_{Asmx}
✗ $NUM_{ac/hr}$

✓ The eight 'checked' descriptors were considered best-performing at all sites and were used to conduct all further analyses.

** %TAA was considered the best performing of the eight, and is used in graphical representations of analysis results.

VOLPE center

U.S. Department of Transportation
Research and Innovative Technology Administration

10

Is there any evidence that visitors respond differently to high altitude jet overflight noise?

Visitors who were exposed to:

- high altitude jet overflight noise only

vs.

- high altitude jet and tour aircraft overflight noise

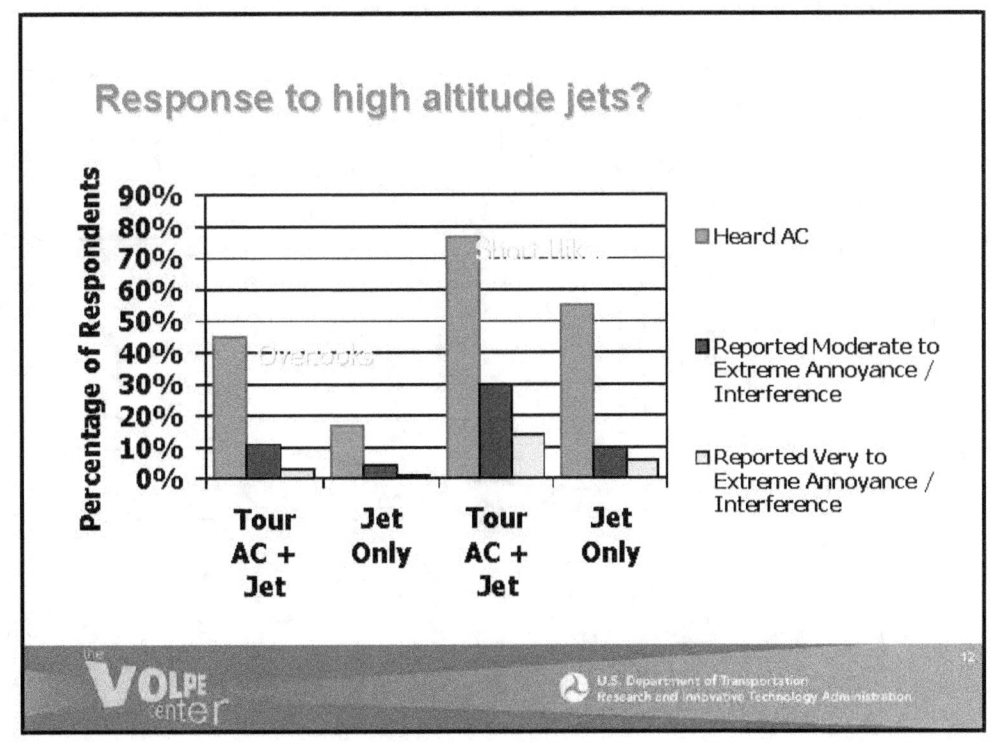

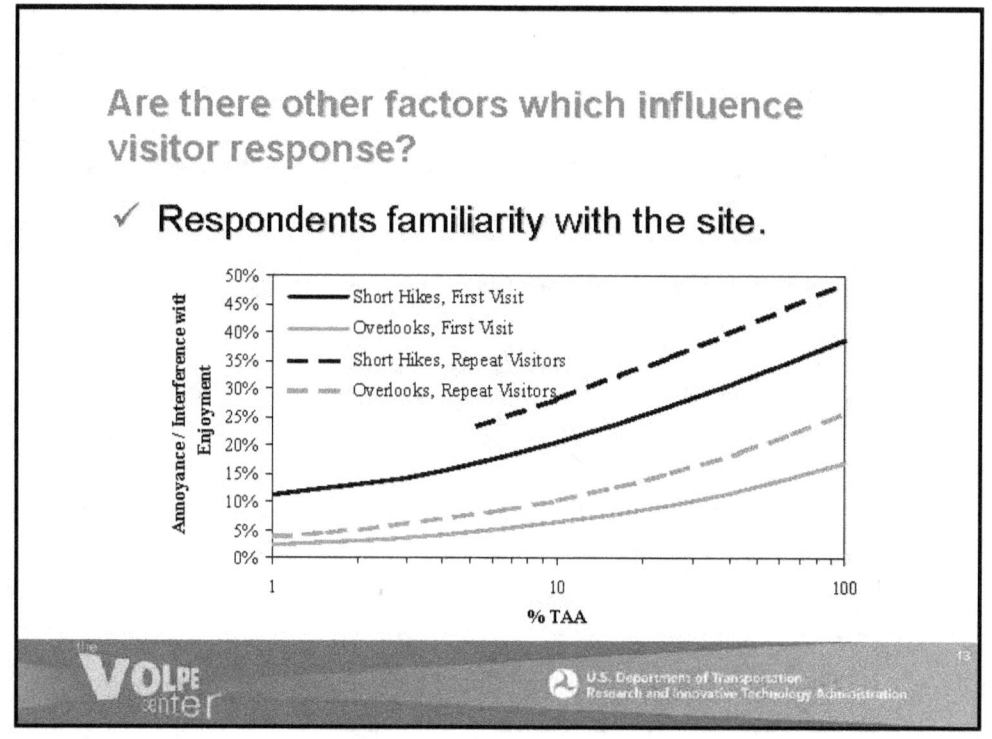

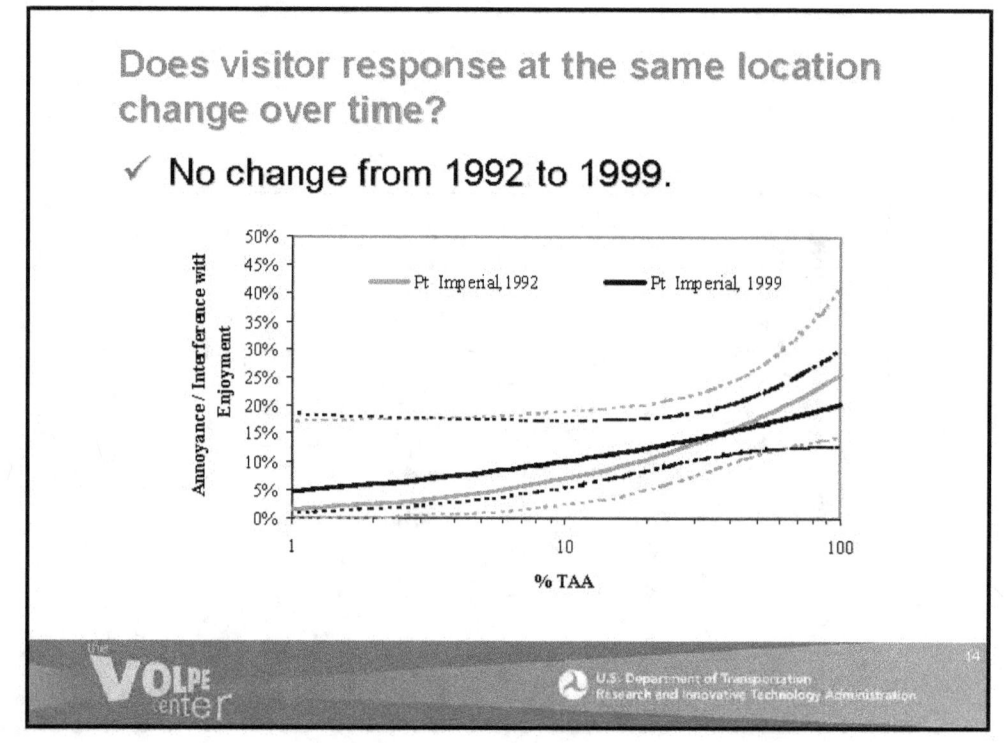

Can the variation in visitor response be explained, not only by acoustic dose, but by site-specific characteristics?

- Site to site similarity (same site type within the same park)

  Are all the overlooks in BCNP similar?

- Park to park similarity (same site type)

  Are the overlooks at BCNP similar to the overlooks at GCNP?

- Site type to site type similarity

  Are overlooks similar to short hikes?

 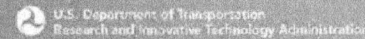

Site to Site Similarity?

All sites of the same type within the same park were found to be similar.

- ✓ BCNP Overlooks: Bryce Point, Rainbow Point, and Fairyland.

- ✓ GCNPSR Overlooks: Pima Point and Lipan Point.

- ✓ GCNPNR Overlooks: Point Imperial 1999 and Point Imperial 1992.

- ✓ BCNP Short Hikes: Queens Garden and Queens Garden Extended.

 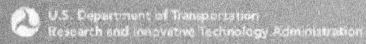

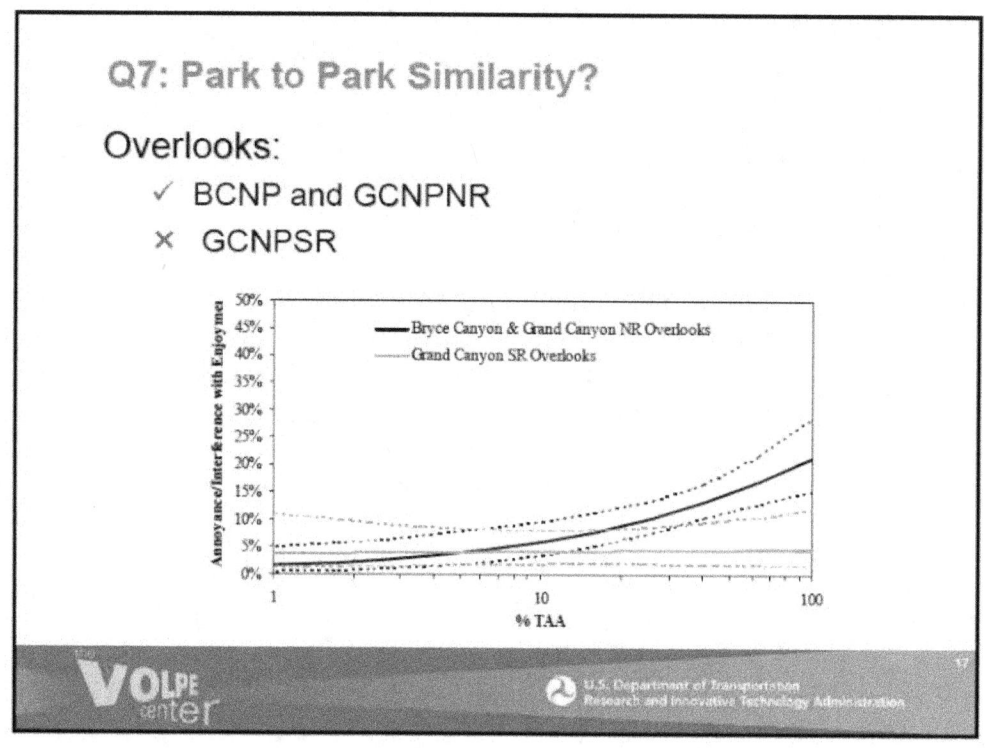

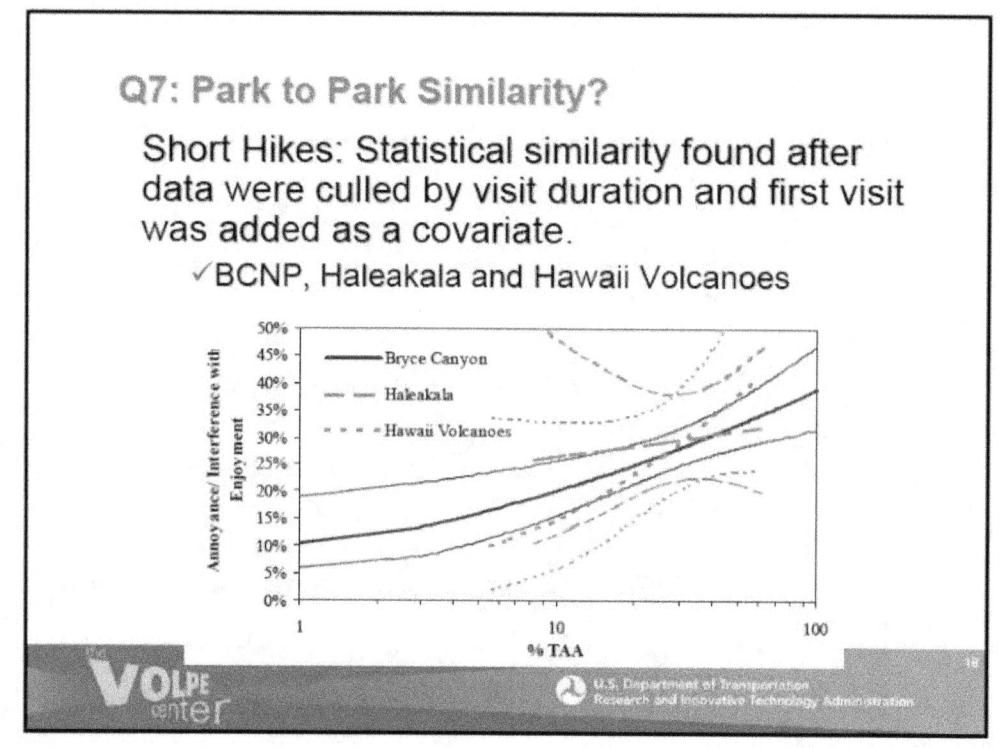

Q8: Site Type to Site Type Similarity?

× Overlooks and short hikes are not statistically similar.

Summary

A large volume of exposure-response data was collected using identical measurement and survey techniques.

- Data is not representative of backcountry areas.
- The data collection methods are difficult to implement in backcountry areas.

Simple exposure-response relationships were developed for use in a National Rule.

- Visitor response may not be 'simple'. Visitor, site, and noise source characteristics may be required to develop strong relationships.

Summary

Visitor response appears to be similar between similar sites at similar parks.

- Knowledge of this is limited – sites / parks covered a limited geographic area.

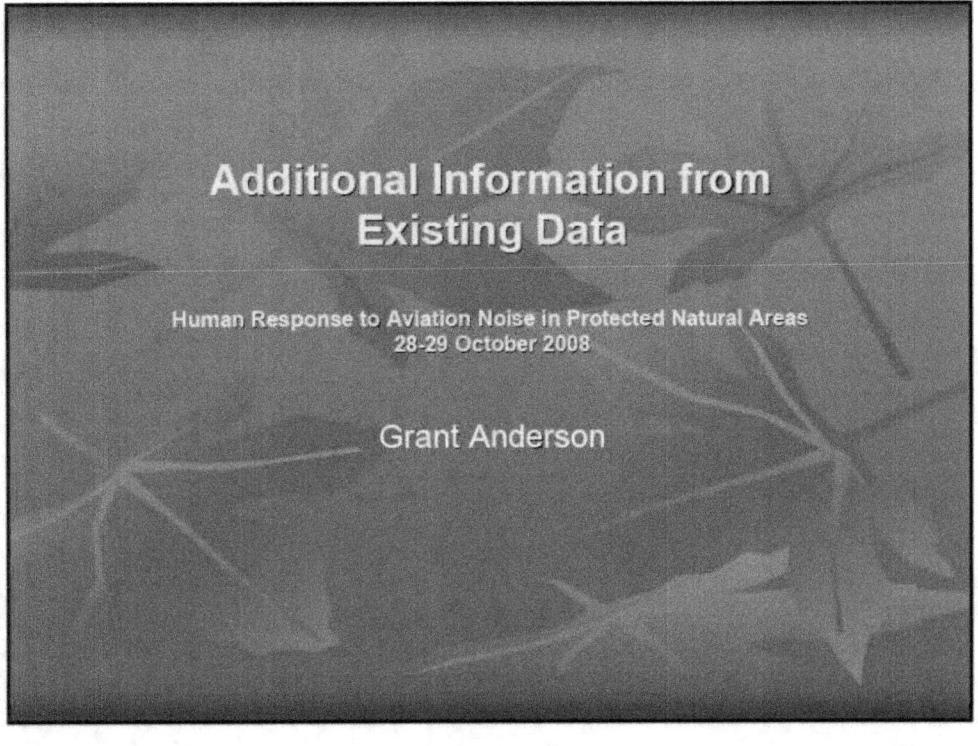

Overview

- Why more analysis?
- Combined database (all parks):
  - Current state
  - Desired augmentation
- Data exploration
- Detailed analysis:
  - Re-do prior regressions: Combined database
  - Improve/expand upon prior methods
- Proposed implementation

Human Response to Aviation Noise in
Protected Natural Areas: 28 October 2008
Slide 1
Additional information from current data
Grant Anderson

Why More Analysis?

- Existing data cost $$$$$.
- Prior analysis on these data:
  - Underfunded
  - Differed by study
- New NPS staff:
  - New ideas
  - Fewer pre-conceptions
- Additional input from technical experts
- **Can be done QUICKLY**

Human Response to Aviation Noise in Protected Natural Areas: 28 October 2008 — Slide 2 — Additional information from current data / Grant Anderson

Combined Database: Current State

- Summarized by Amanda and Nick:
  - Grand Canyon (2 years), Haleakala, Hawaii Volcanoes, Bryce Canyon, White Sands
  - 2 visitor responses (different dichotomizations)
  - 10-15 acoustic doses
  - 20-30 mediators (some dichotomized)
- All in Statistica/Excel format:
  - One row per visitor
  - One column per variable
  - Examples on next slide
- Analyzed with dichotomized logistic regression

Human Response to Aviation Noise in Protected Natural Areas: 28 October 2008 — Slide 3 — Additional information from current data / Grant Anderson

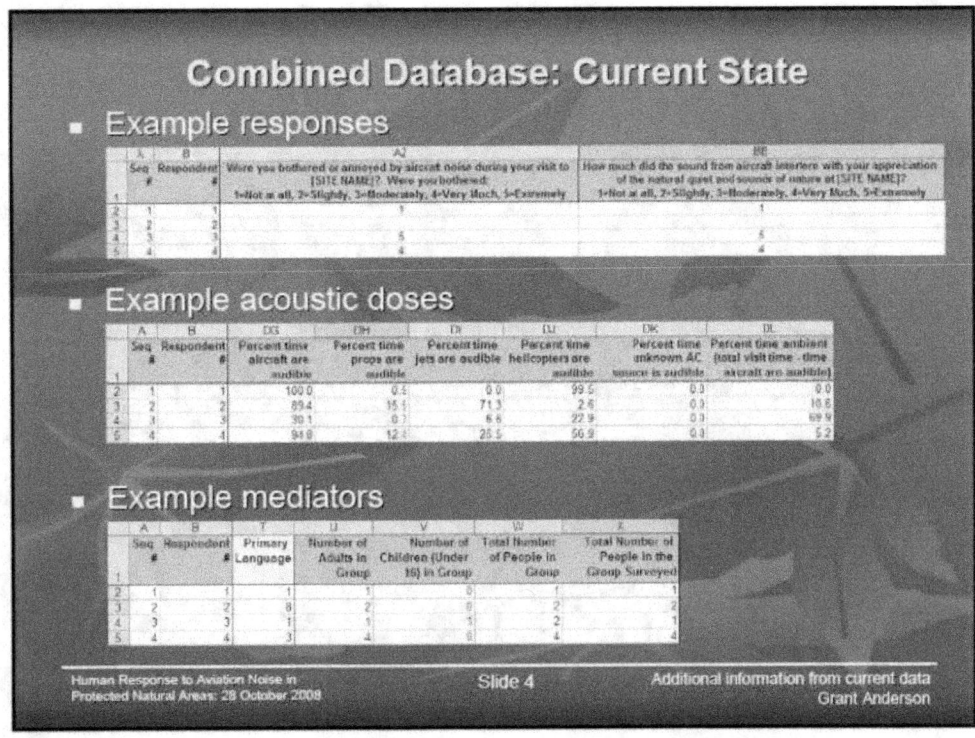

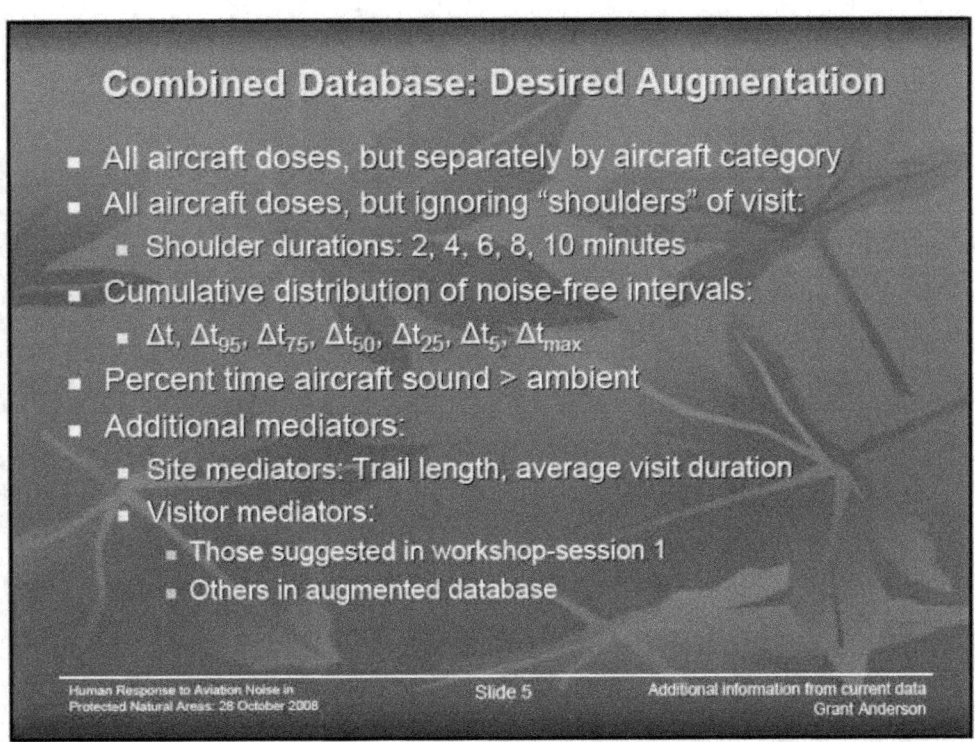

Data Exploration

- Purpose: Avoid potential confounding
- Correlation coefficients:
  - All mixtures of doses, responses, mediators
  - Retain "ordinal" categories (prior to dichotomization)
- Square matrix plots
- Box plots: All variables
- Categorized scatterplots:
  - All responses vs all doses, categorized by:
    - Type of site
    - Specific site
    - Other relevant mediators

Human Response to Aviation Noise in
Protected Natural Areas: 28 October 2008   Slide 6   Additional information from current data
Grant Anderson

Detailed Analysis: Re-do Prior Regressions

- Combined database, for uniform analysis
- Dichotomize between:
  - Slightly and Moderately (previous HMMH)
  - Moderately and Very (previous Volpe)
- Try "cumulative" logistic regression for greater power
- Use mediator hierarchy, not step-wise regression

Human Response to Aviation Noise in
Protected Natural Areas: 28 October 2008   Slide 7   Additional information from current data
Grant Anderson

Detailed Analysis: Improve/Expand

- Augmented doses, mediators from above
- Additional dose improvements:
  - Compound doses: Allow more than one into regression
  - Combine % time audible and how loud *when audible*
  - Try dose satisfying:
    - Low S/N: Dominated by S/N ratio
    - High S/N: Dominated by Signal
  - Try dose that includes fluctuations: Aircraft Leq <u>and</u> StDev?
  - Compare linear and logarithmic dose scales

Human Response to Aviation Noise in Protected Natural Areas: 28 October 2008   Slide 8   Additional information from current data   Grant Anderson

Detailed Analysis: Improve/Expand

- Generalized logistic form (5-parameter Kappa distribution) for doses and selected mediators

Skew left or right   *Lower limits on dose*

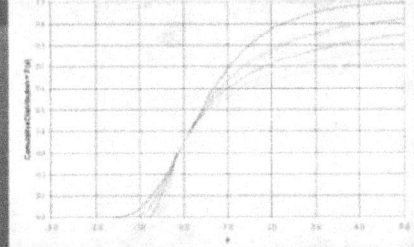

Both can have upper-response limit less than 100%

Human Response to Aviation Noise in Protected Natural Areas: 28 October 2008   Slide 9   Additional information from current data   Grant Anderson

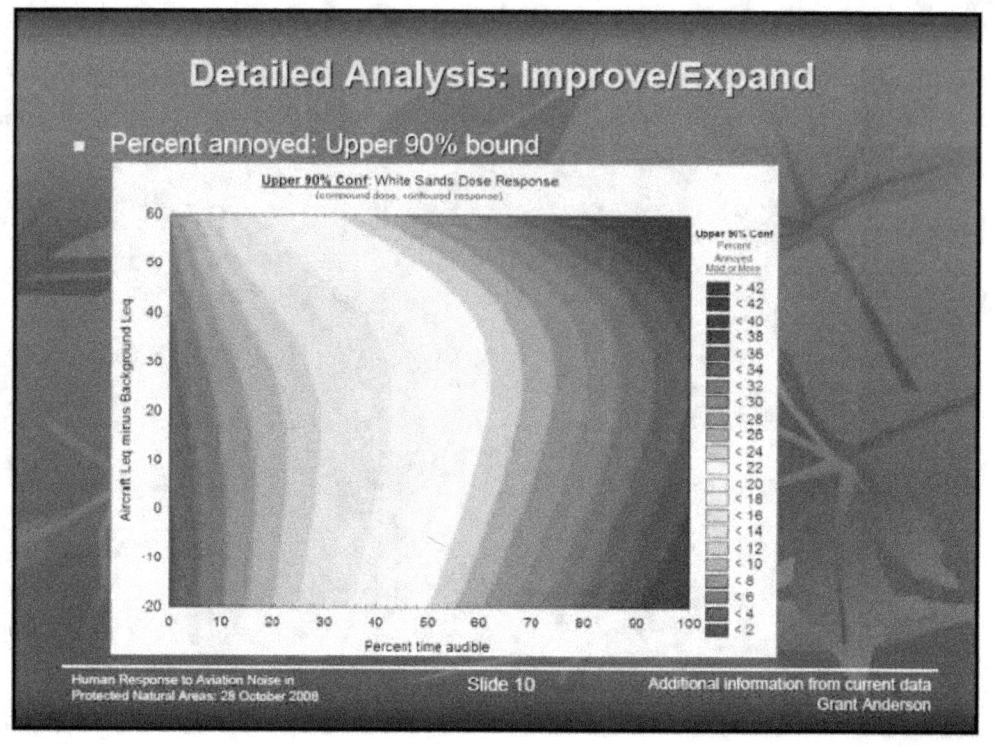

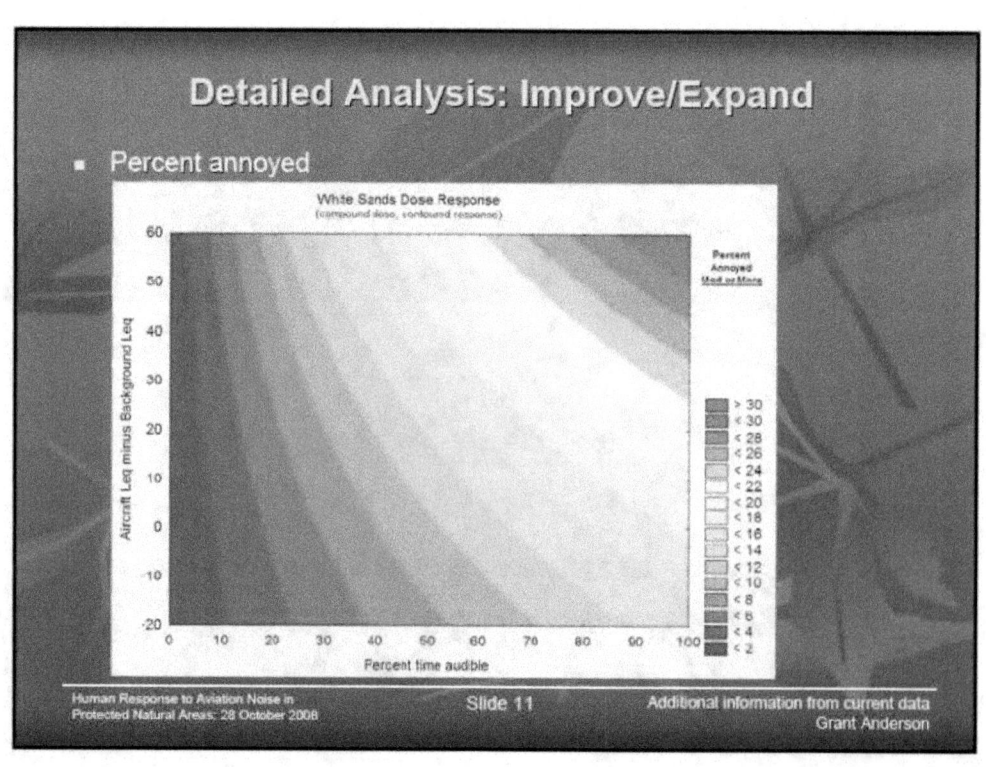

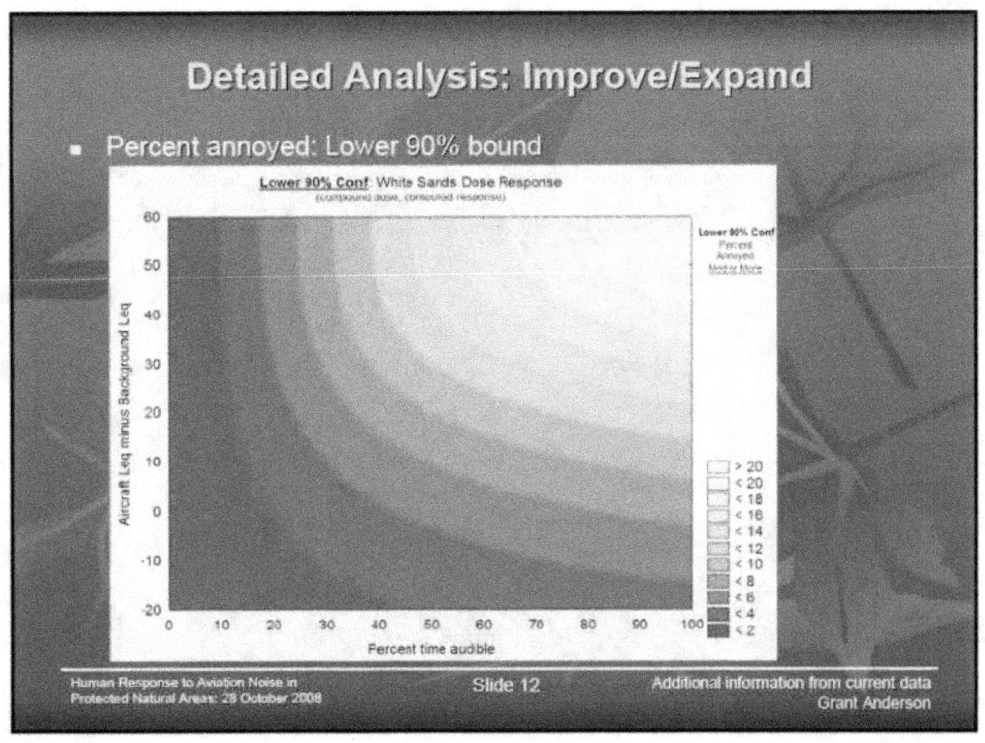

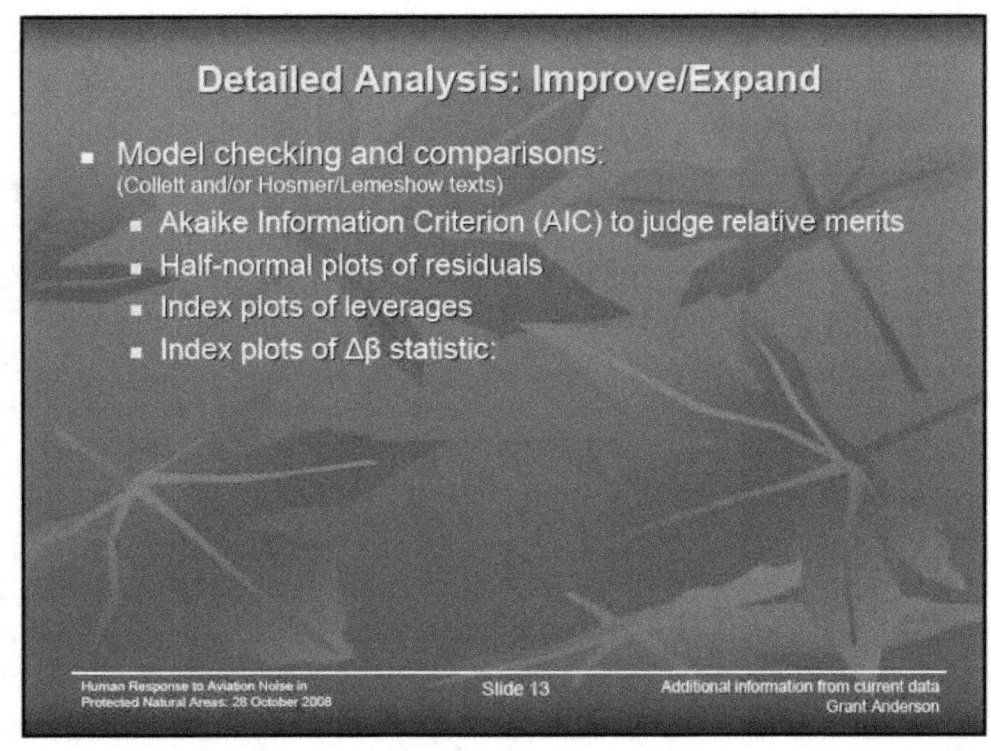

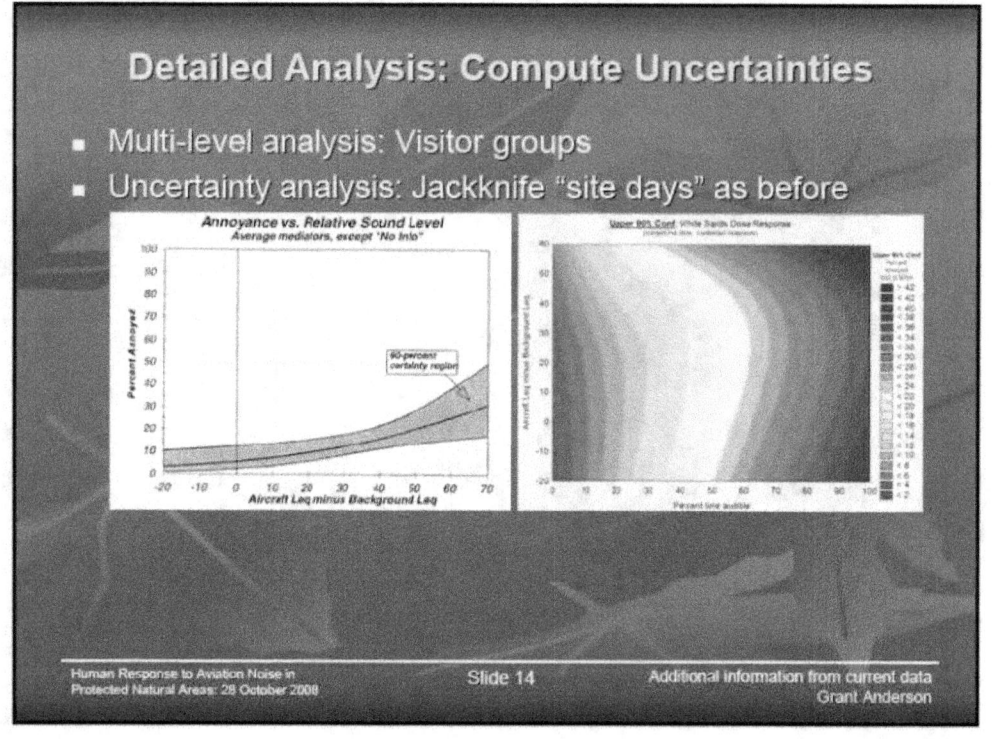

Proposed Implementation

Mine Additional Information from Existing Data

- Augment existing database:
  - Ignore "shoulders"
  - Noise-free intervals
  - Percent time aircraft sound > ambient
  - Additional site and visitor mediators
- Explore the combined data: Tables and graphs
- Perform detailed analysis:
  - Re-do prior regressions with uniform methods
  - Improve/expand upon prior methods
  - Compute sampling uncertainties
- ≈ $110,000

Human Response to Aviation Noise in
Protected Natural Areas: 28 October 2008

Slide 15

Additional information from current data
Grant Anderson

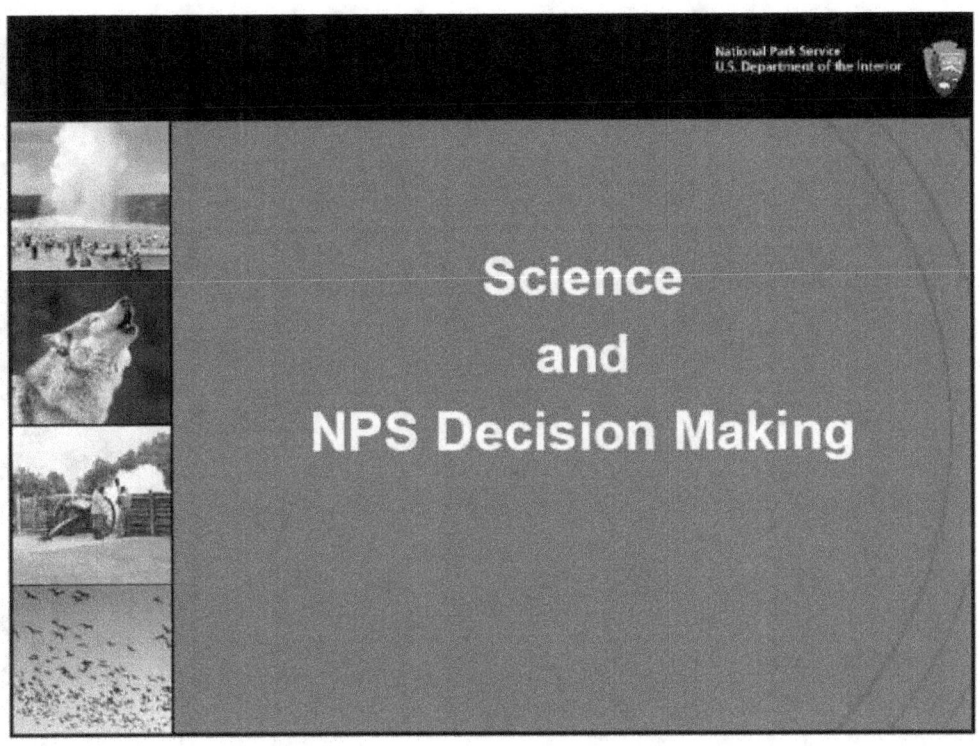

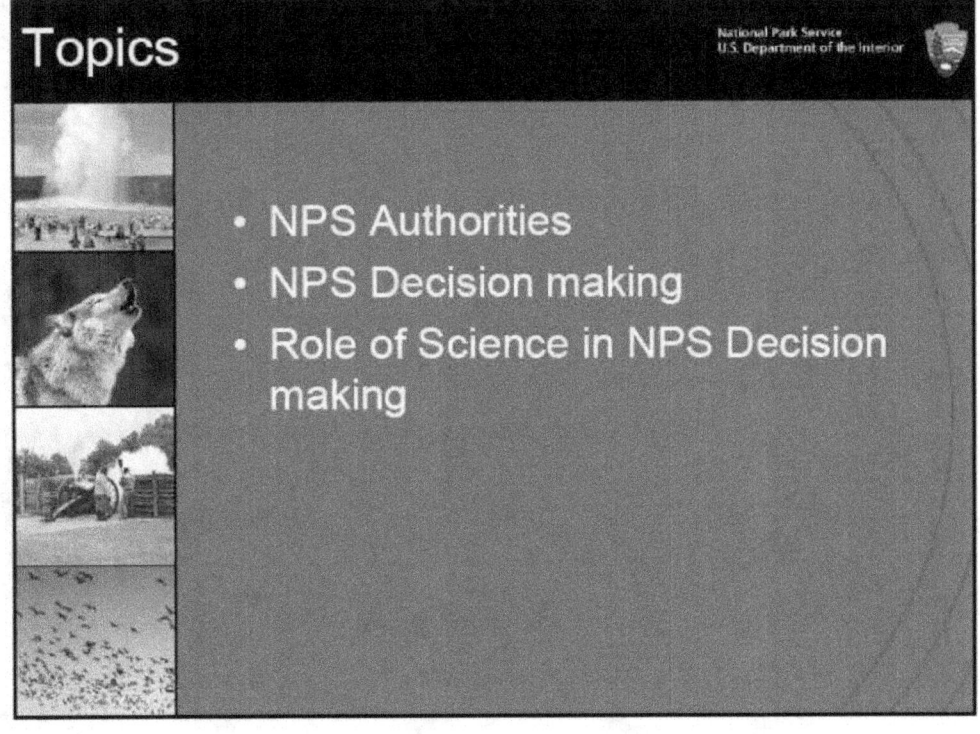

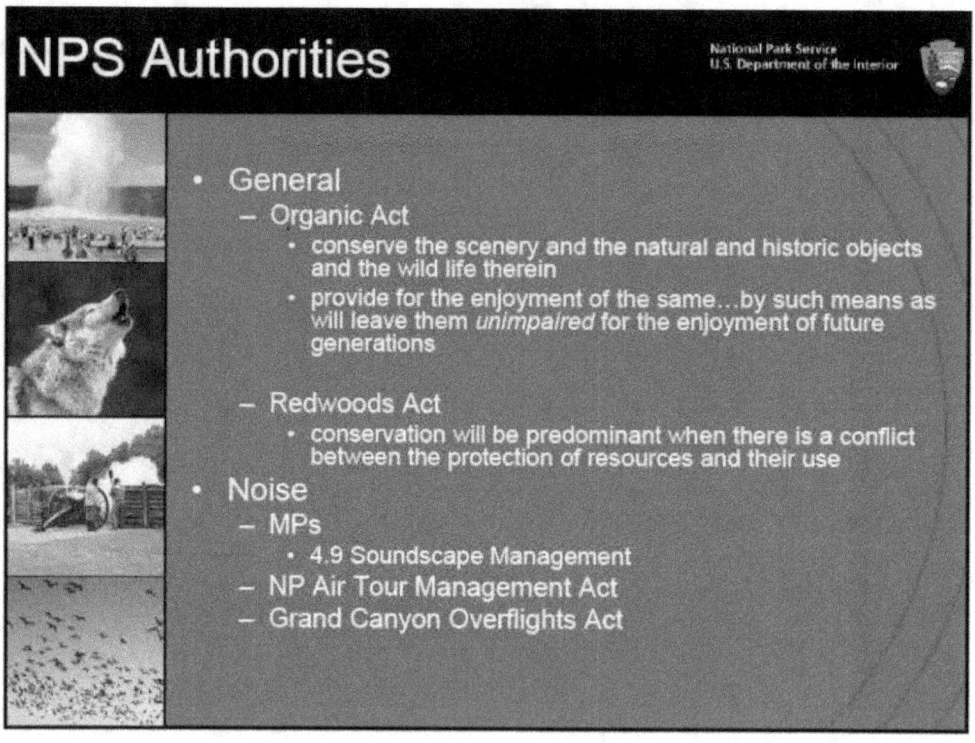

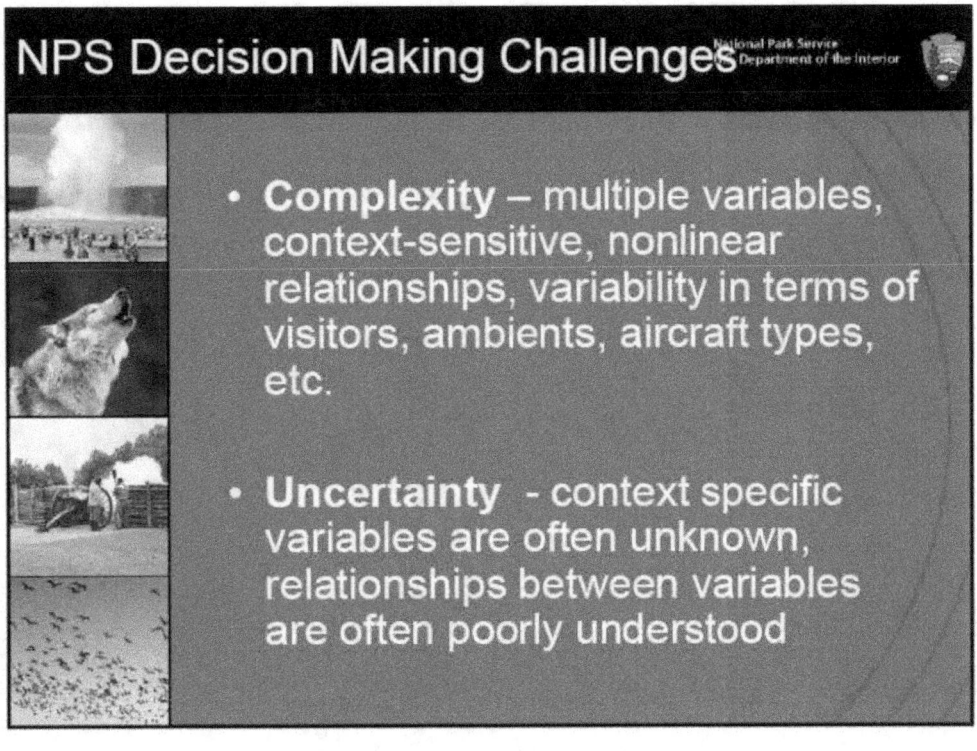

NPS Decision Making Challenges National Park Service Department of the Interior

- **Complexity** – multiple variables, context-sensitive, nonlinear relationships, variability in terms of visitors, ambients, aircraft types, etc.

- **Uncertainty** - context specific variables are often unknown, relationships between variables are often poorly understood

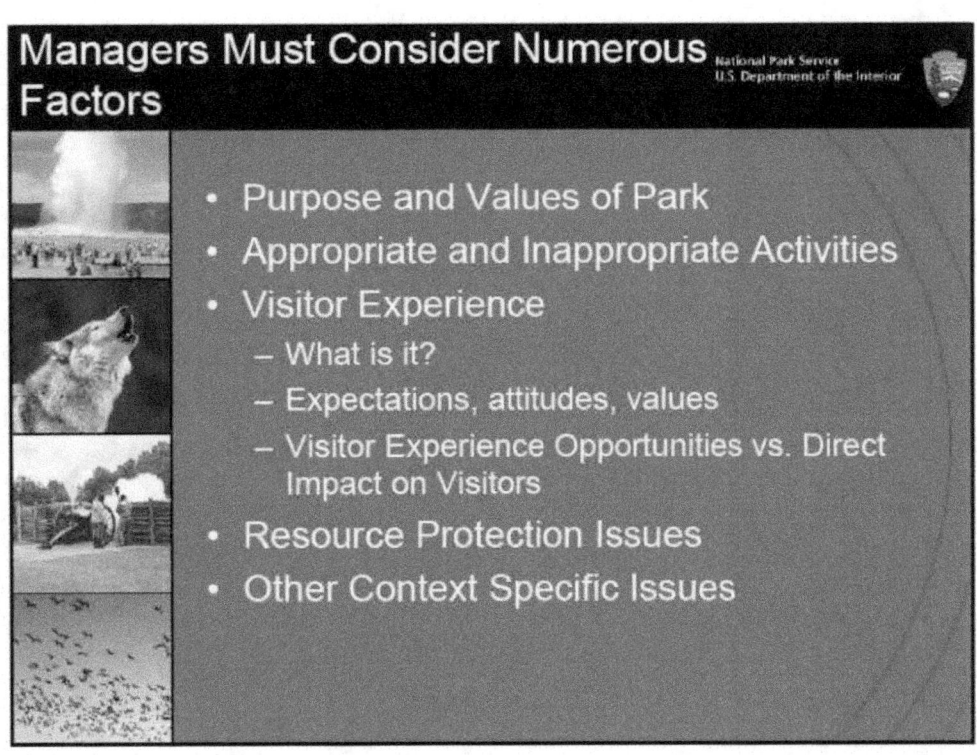

Managers Must Consider Numerous Factors National Park Service U.S. Department of the Interior

- Purpose and Values of Park
- Appropriate and Inappropriate Activities
- Visitor Experience
  - What is it?
  - Expectations, attitudes, values
  - Visitor Experience Opportunities vs. Direct Impact on Visitors
- Resource Protection Issues
- Other Context Specific Issues

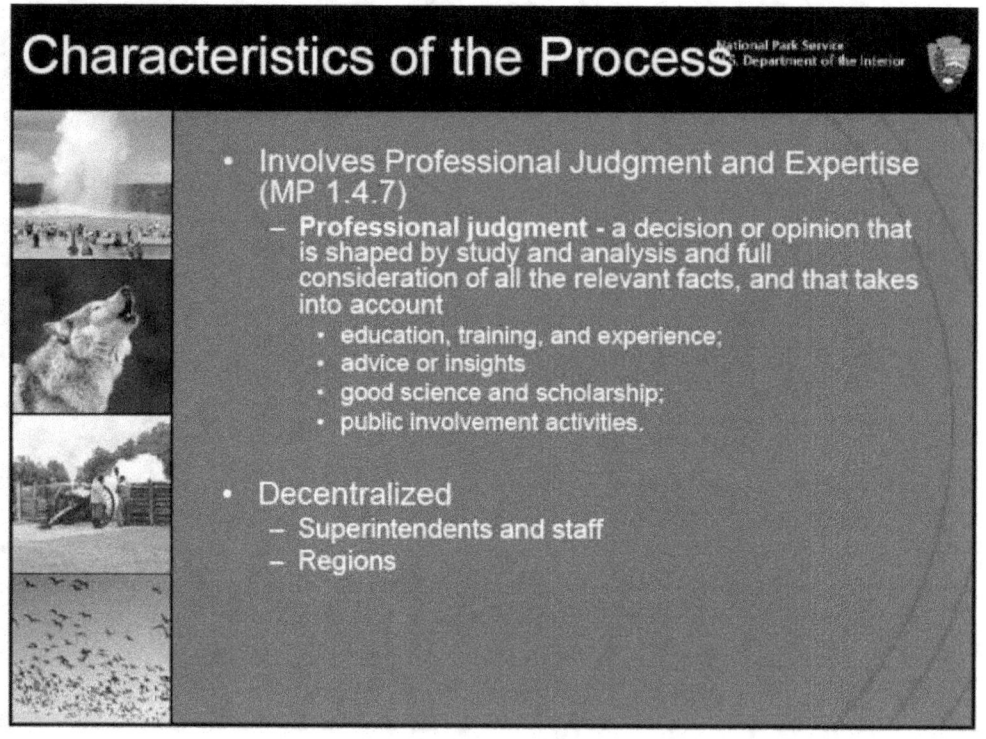

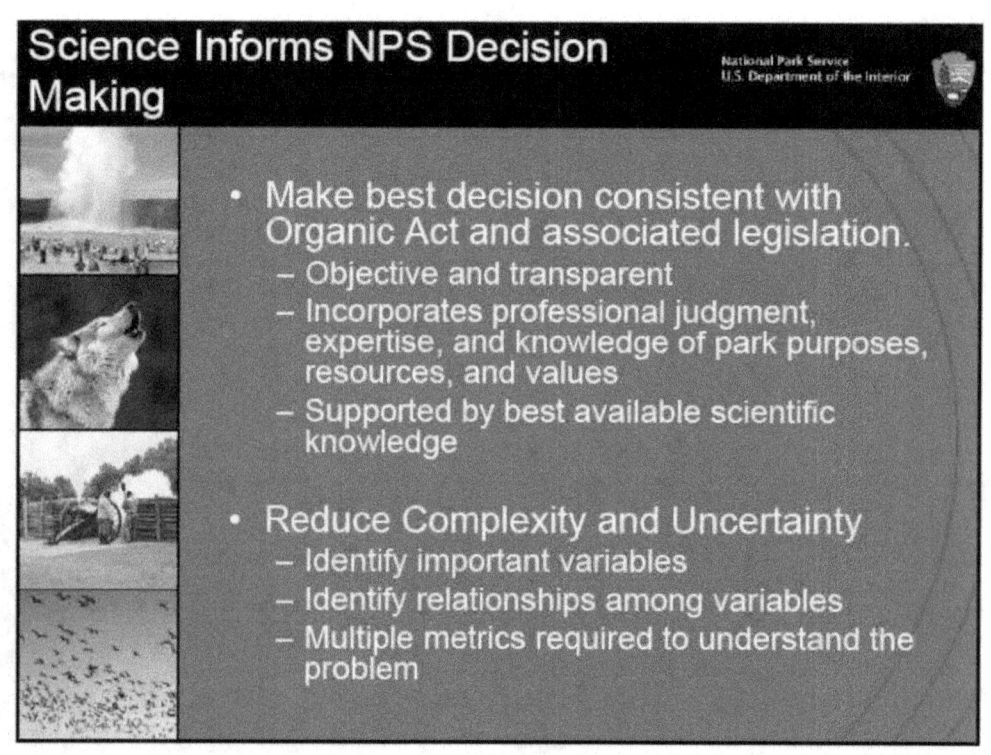

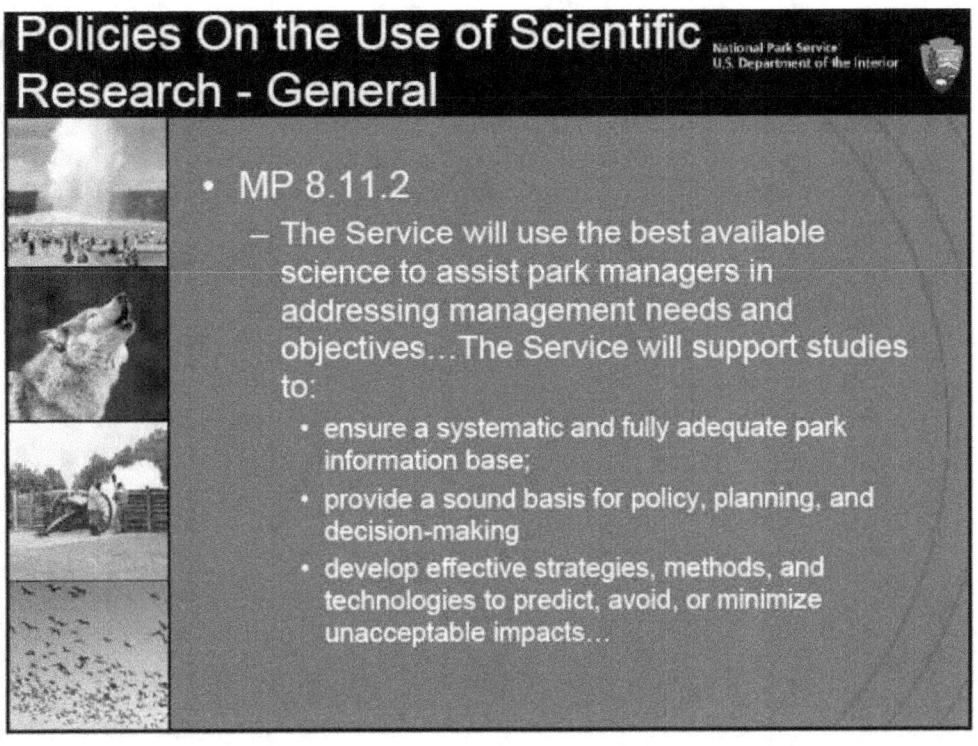

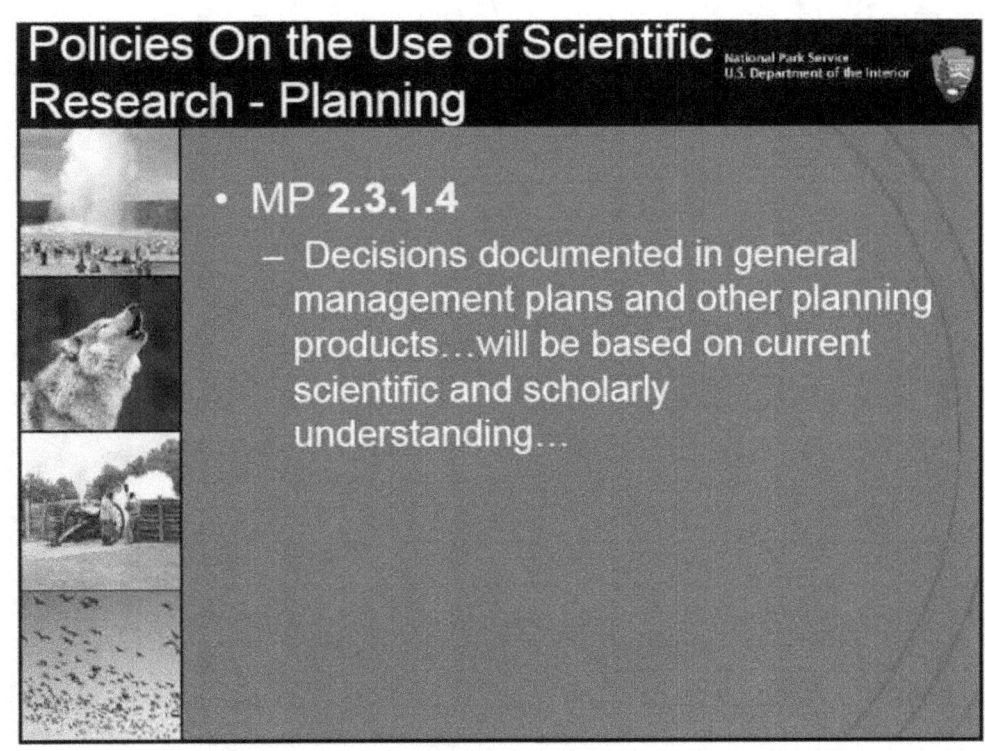

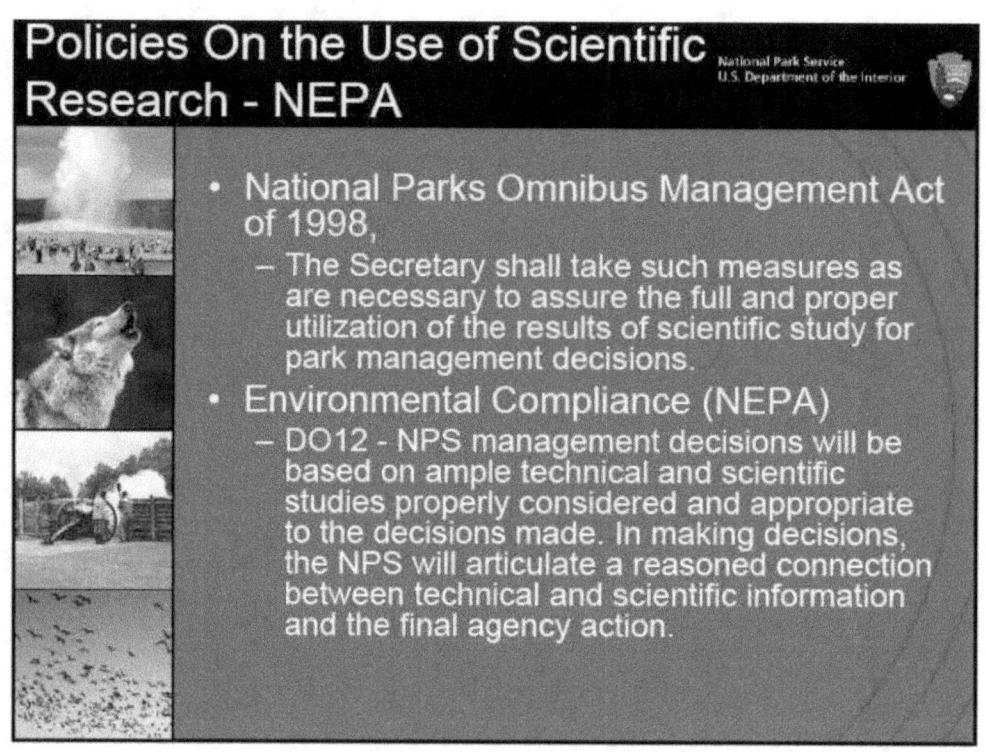

Policies On the Use of Scientific Research - NEPA

National Park Service
U.S. Department of the Interior

- National Parks Omnibus Management Act of 1998,
  - The Secretary shall take such measures as are necessary to assure the full and proper utilization of the results of scientific study for park management decisions.
- Environmental Compliance (NEPA)
  - DO12 - NPS management decisions will be based on ample technical and scientific studies properly considered and appropriate to the decisions made. In making decisions, the NPS will articulate a reasoned connection between technical and scientific information and the final agency action.

Human Dimensions of Park Soundscapes: Recent Research and Recommendations for Future Directions Part I

Robert Manning

Rubenstein School of Environment and Natural Resources

University of Vermont

Human Response to Aviation Noise in Protected Natural Areas Workshop, October 28-29, 2008, Boston, MA

Outline

- Park and Outdoor Recreation Management Frameworks
- Application to Human-caused Noise
- Program of Research at Muir Woods National Monument
- Future Research

Park and Outdoor Recreation Management Frameworks

- Limits of Acceptable Change (LAC)
- Visitor Experience and Resource Protection (VERP)

Outline of Frameworks

1. Formulate management objectives/desired conditions and associated indicators and standards of quality
2. Monitor indicators of quality
3. Apply management practices to maintain standards of quality

Application to Human-caused Noise

- Muir Woods National Monument, California

Indicators of Quality

- Qualitative methods
- Quantitative methods

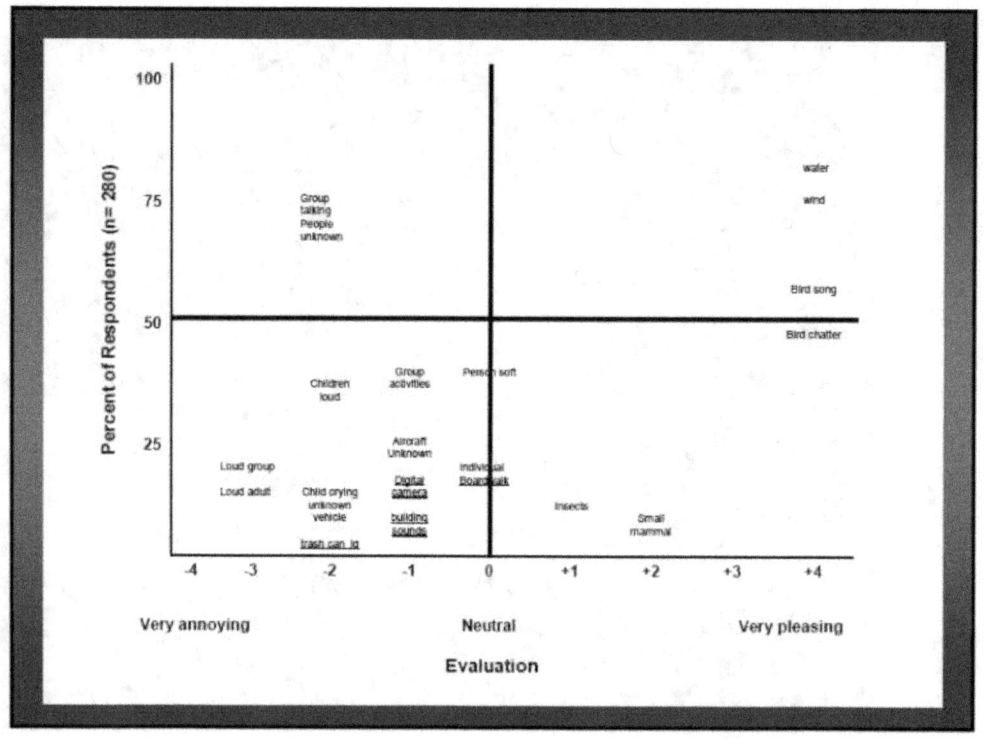

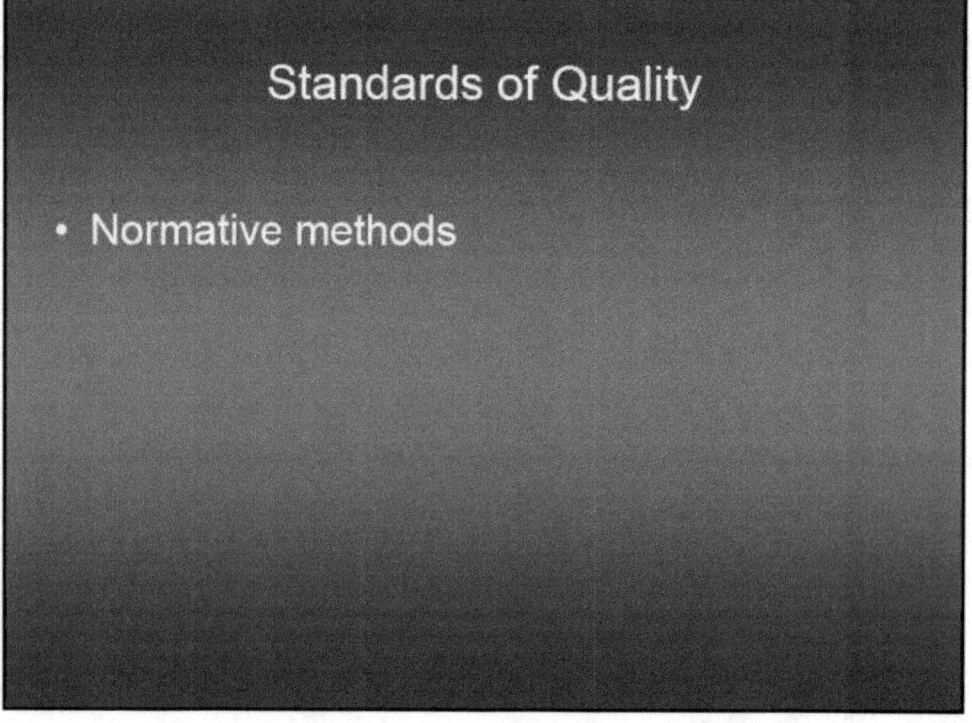

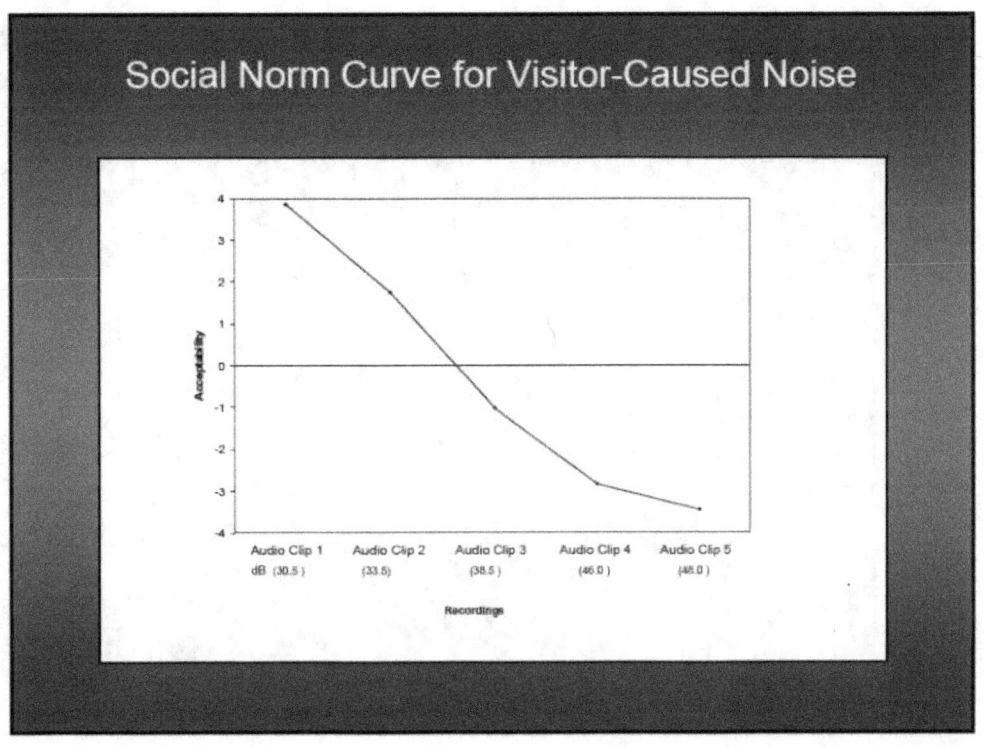

Monitoring

- NPS Natural Sounds Program
- Visitor surveys

Management

- Experimental approach
- "Quiet zone" and "quiet days"
- Significant reduction in visitor-caused noise
- Significant increase in visitor behaviors designed to reduce noise
- Visitors highly supportive of management actions

Future Research

- Refinement of Muir Woods/VERP approach
- Extension to other sources of human-caused noise
- A normative model of human-caused noise

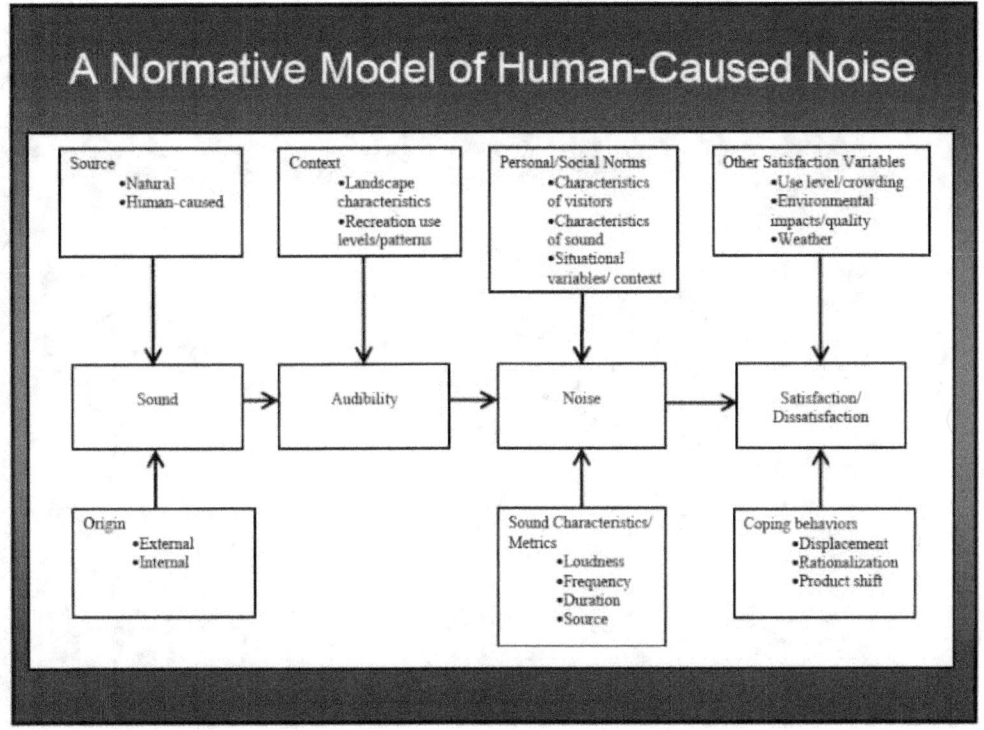

Future Research

• Refinement of Muir Woods/VERP approach
• Extension to other sources of human-caused noise
• A normative model of human-caused noise
• Natural and cultural sounds as an enhancement to the visitor experience

Human Dimensions of Park Soundscapes: Recent Research and Recommendations for Future Directions - Part II

Steve Lawson, Ph.D.
Virginia Tech / Resource Systems Group, Inc.

Background

- ~10 years NPS research

- NPS/CSU workshops in 2006 & 2007

- Soundscape-related visitor surveys – HALE, HAVO, GRSM

- Visitor use and noise modeling studies – ROMO & GRSM

- GWS/ISSRM conference sessions; Park Science

Effects of Air Tour Noise on Visitors' Experiences
Haleakala and Hawaii Volcanoes National Parks

- Summer, 2007
- HALE: Kipahulu and Haleakala Crater
- HAVO: Steam Vents and Trail to Thurston Lava Tube
- Audio Recordings & Attended Listening Surveys
- Indicator-based adaptive management

Haleakala and Hawaii Volcanoes National Parks
Attended Listening Survey

- Visitor-based inventory of sounds (~30 listed)

- Acceptability & personal interpretation

- Feelings/emotions

- Presence/absence of aircraft documented by surveyor

Sample Size and Response Rate
Attended Listening Survey

Location	Sample Size	Response Rate
Trail to Waimoku Falls	193	94.6%
Sliding Sands Trail	161	91.0%

Aircraft-related Findings
Attended Listening Survey

Location	Heard Aircraft	Acceptability	Personal Interpretation
Trail to Waimoku Falls	55%	-0.4	-1.0
Sliding Sands Trail	63%	-0.3	-0.9

NOTE: Acceptability scale ranged from -4 "Very Unacceptable" to +4 "Very Acceptable".
Personal interpretation scale ranged from -4 "Very Annoying" to +4 "Very Pleasing"

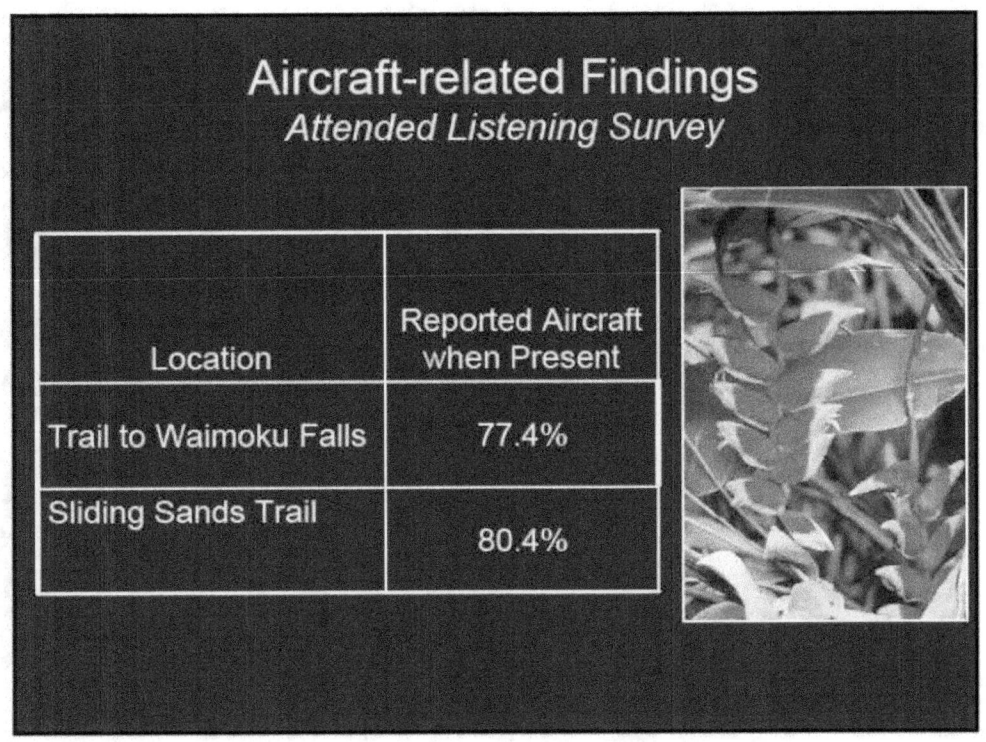

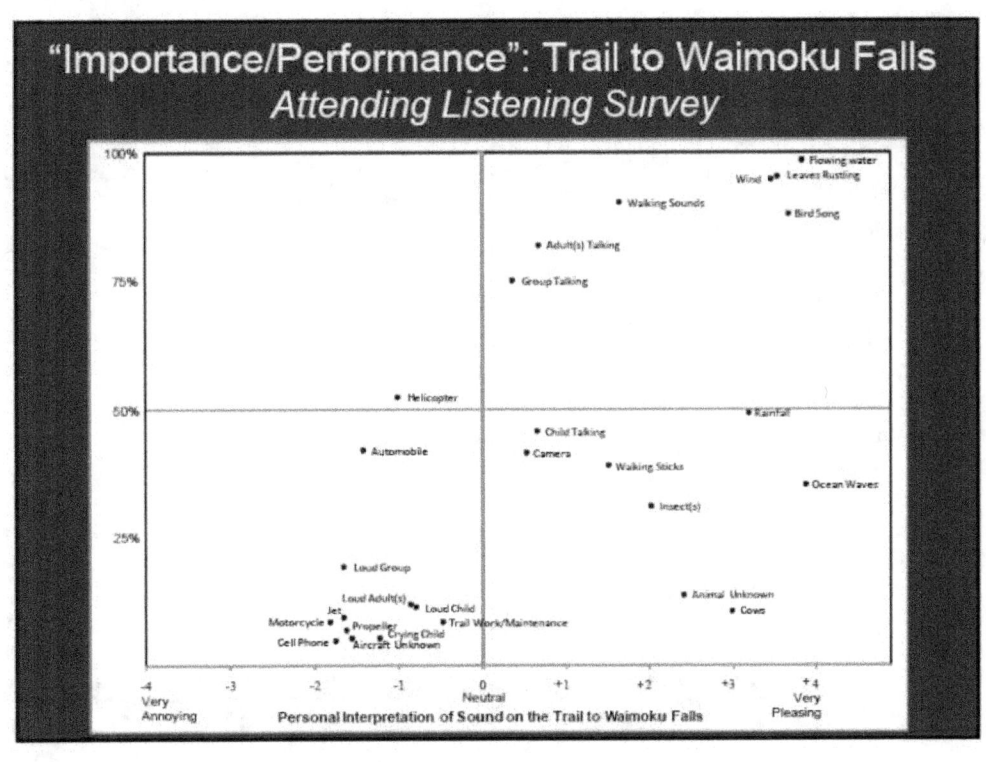

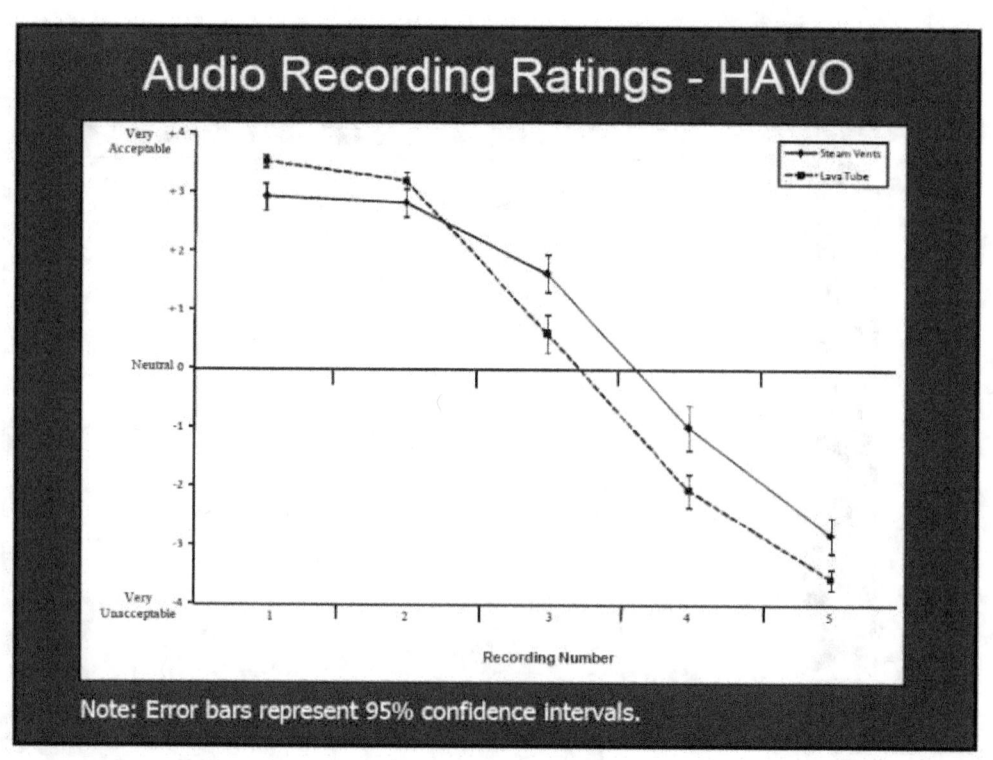

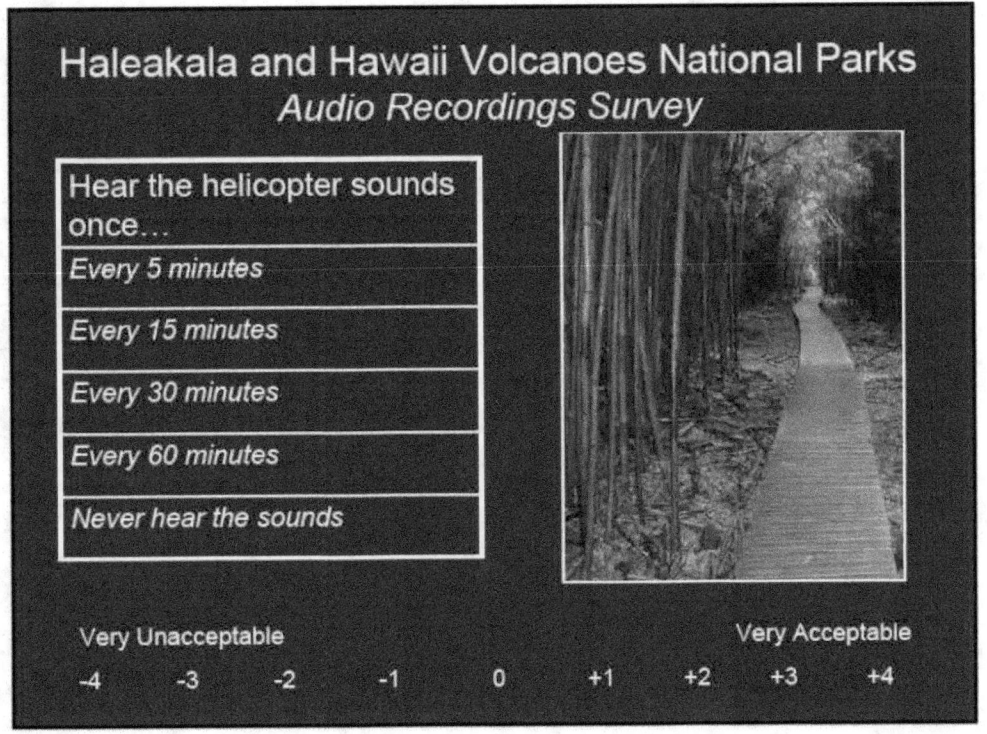

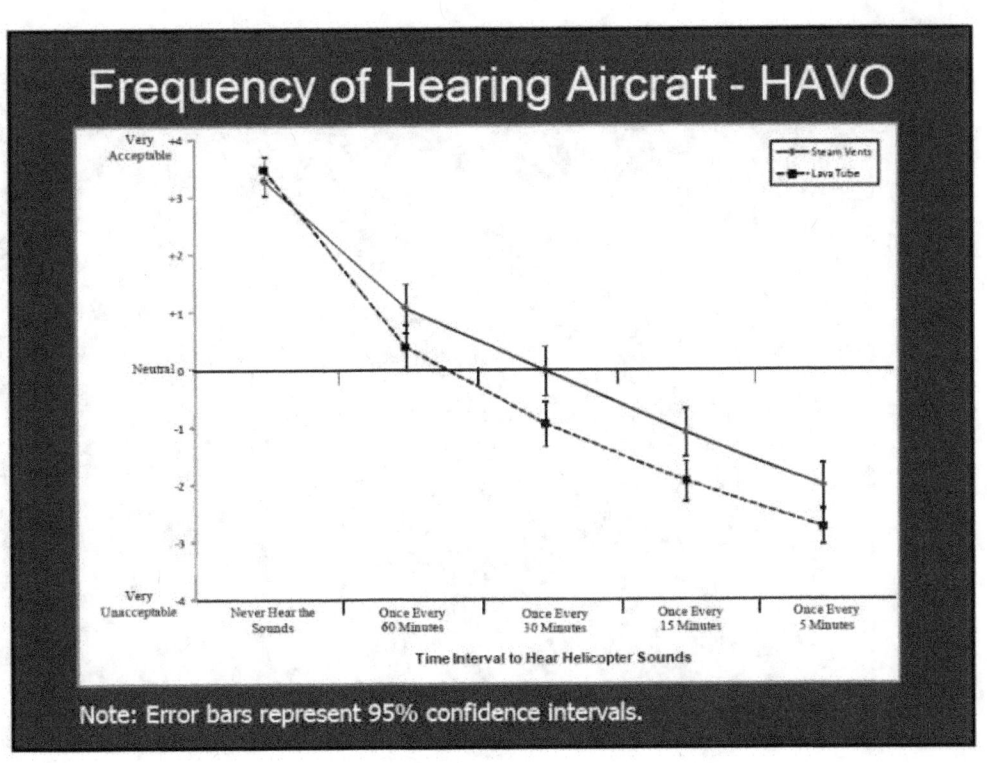

Audio Recordings Response Rate

Location	Sample Size	Response Rate
Steam Vents	182	55.8%
Thurston Lava Tube	192	68.3%
Trail to Waimoku Falls	303	64.1%

Haleakala and Hawaii Volcanoes National Parks
Summary of Findings

- Notice helicopters when asked to pay attention to park sounds

- Importance/Performance suggests immediate attention warranted

- Audio clip results include visitor-based standards
  - Event-based and audibility-based

- Visitors generally consider exposure more than once per hour unacceptable

Haleakala Wilderness Visitor Survey

- 2007 backcountry camping and cabin permittees

- Mail survey, April – June, 2008

- 61.9% response rate, 419 complete

- 52% reported hearing aircraft during their trip

Haleakala Wilderness Visitor Survey
Soundscape-related Findings

Experiencing the sounds of nature was...

...the most important reason for taking an overnight trip in the Haleakala Wilderness

...the second most commonly cited factor contributing to visitors' sense of being in wilderness (open-ended)

The sights and/or sounds of aircraft were...

...the most commonly cited factor detracting from visitors' sense of being in wilderness (open-ended)

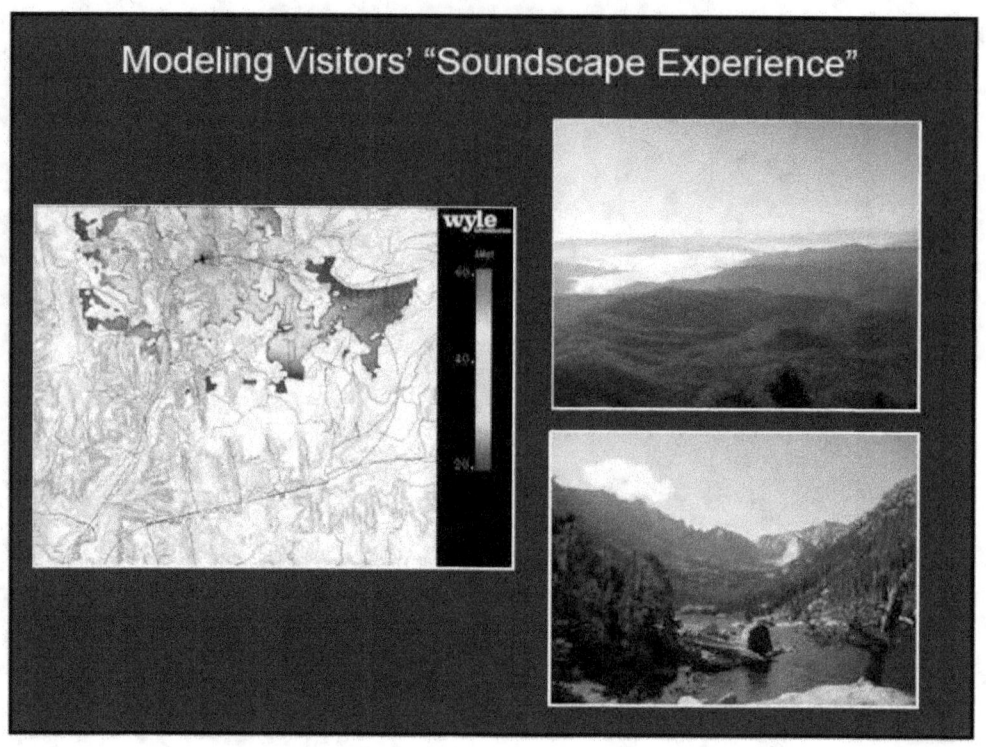

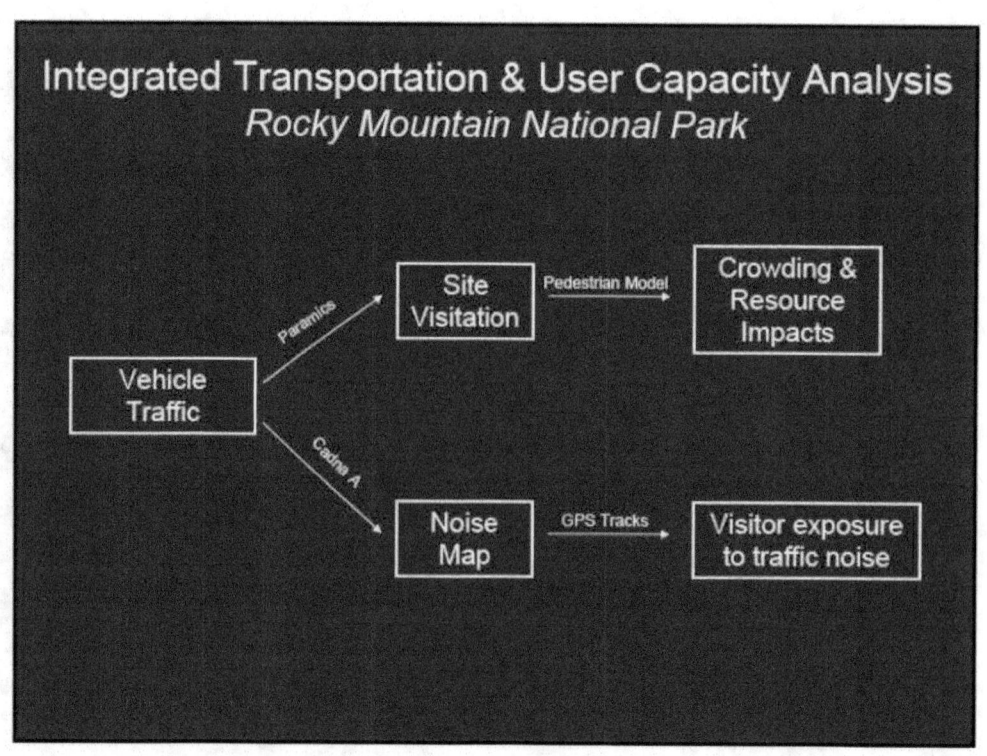

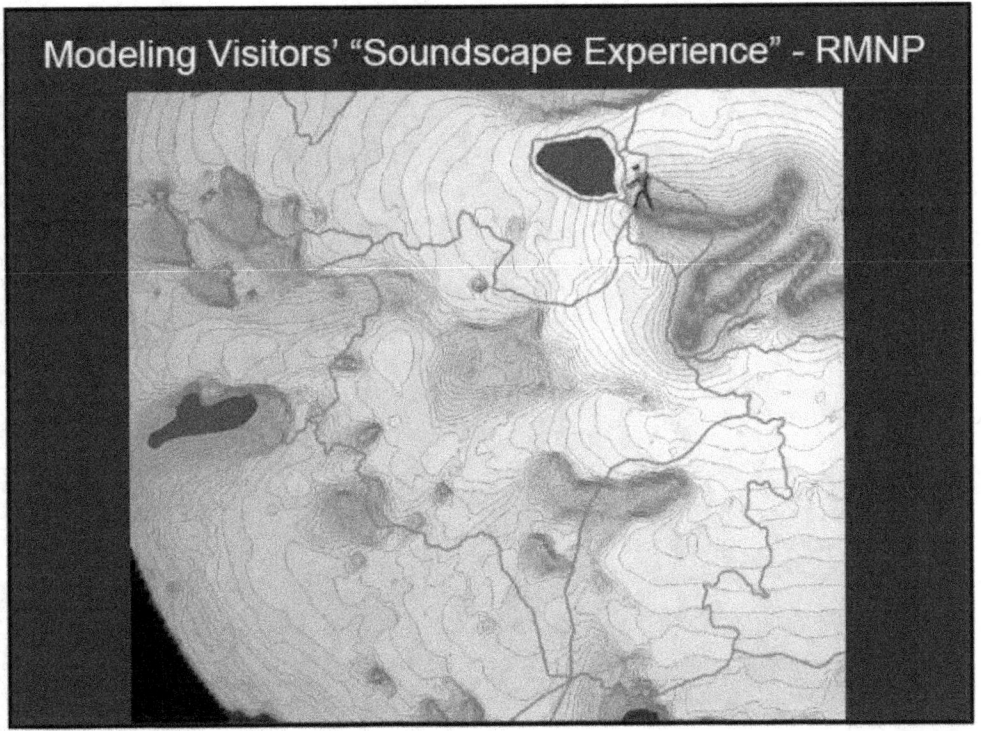

Modeling Visitors' "Soundscape Experience" - RMNP

Recommendations for Future Directions

1. Evaluation of context in "dose-response" studies

- Visitor populations – e.g., air tour participants

- Setting – e.g., wilderness v. frontcountry (GRSM, HALE)

- Noise source – e.g., military/air tour/commercial jet; vehicle traffic v. aviation v. personal electronics

- Type of NPS unit

Recommendations for Future Directions (cont.)

2. Measurement of visitor standards for event-based indicators

3. Integration of visitor use and aviation noise modeling; locate & quantify noise exposure, by type & amount of use

4. Tradeoff analyses of management alternatives

   - State choice modeling; on-market valuation of natural sounds/quiet

Recommendations for Future Directions (cont.)

5. In situ studies of soundscape experience & evaluation

   - GPS and portable recording devices

6. Visual-based assessments of high-altitude flights

Relative Importance Of Attributes

Relative importance	Attribute	Wald test
1st	Visitor-caused damage to vegetation & soils	$\chi^2 = 452.22$, $p < .001$
2nd	Public access	$\chi^2 = 166.01$, $p = .024$
3rd	People off-trail on vegetation & soils	$\chi^2 = 156.75$, $p < .001$
4th	Structures to minimize off-trail hiking	$\chi^2 = 57.20$, $p < .001$
5th	Freedom of travel	$\chi^2 = 26.13$, $p < .001$
6th	People on trail	$\chi^2 = 7.79$, $p = .02$

Predicted Support for Management Alternatives

Attributes	"Hands-off" Management	Visitor Education	Site Management	Limit Use
Access	None turned away	None turned away	None turned away	Many turned away
Freedom	Allowed to roam off-trail	Encouraged to stay on paved trail or rock surfaces	Required to stay on paved trail	Encouraged to stay on paved trail or rock surfaces
Structures	No mgmt. structures	Signs	Fencing	Signs
People on trail	Many other visitors	Many other visitors	Many other visitors	Few other visitors
People off-trail	Many visitors off-trail	Some visitors off-trail	No visitors off-trail	No visitors off-trail
Vegetation & soil damage	Extensive	Some	Little	Little
Relative Support	2.3%	33.1%	45.0%	19.6%

Human Dimensions of Park Soundscapes: Recent Research and Recommendations for Future Directions

Britton Mace, Ph.D.
Associate Professor
Department of Psychology
Southern Utah University
Cedar City, UT 84720
(435) 865-8569
mace@suu.edu

Background

- I began working in landscape perception with the National Park Service in 1993.
  - visibility projects led to researching overflights in parks

- My training and methodological approach is based on experimental social and environmental psychology.

- Laboratory studies employ protocols developed in landscape evaluation and aesthetics.

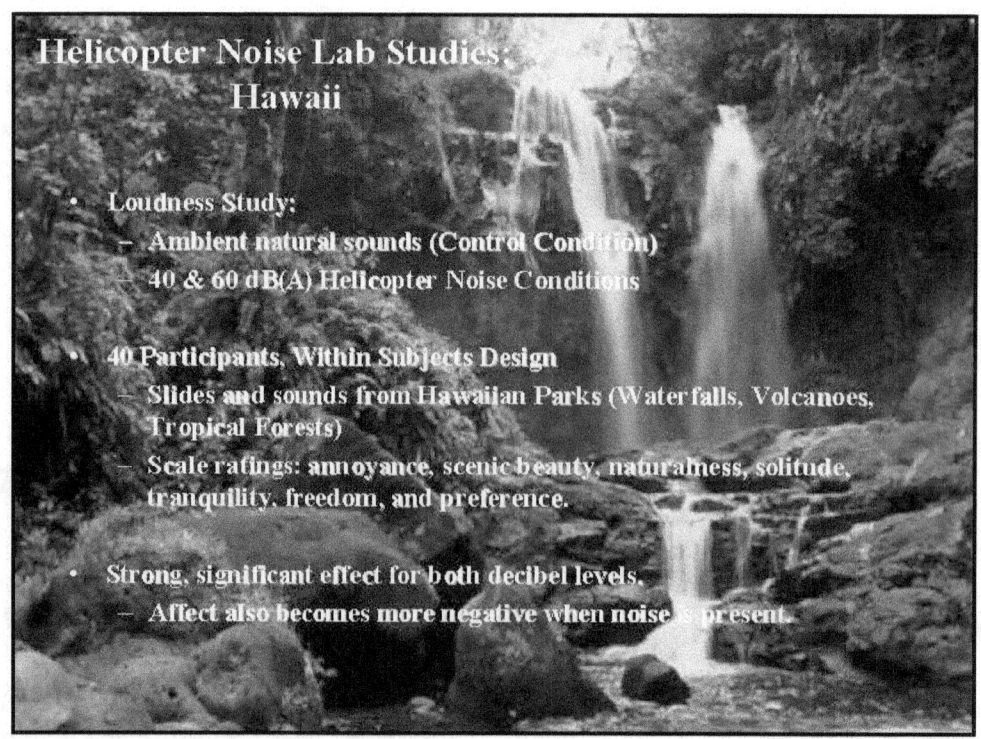

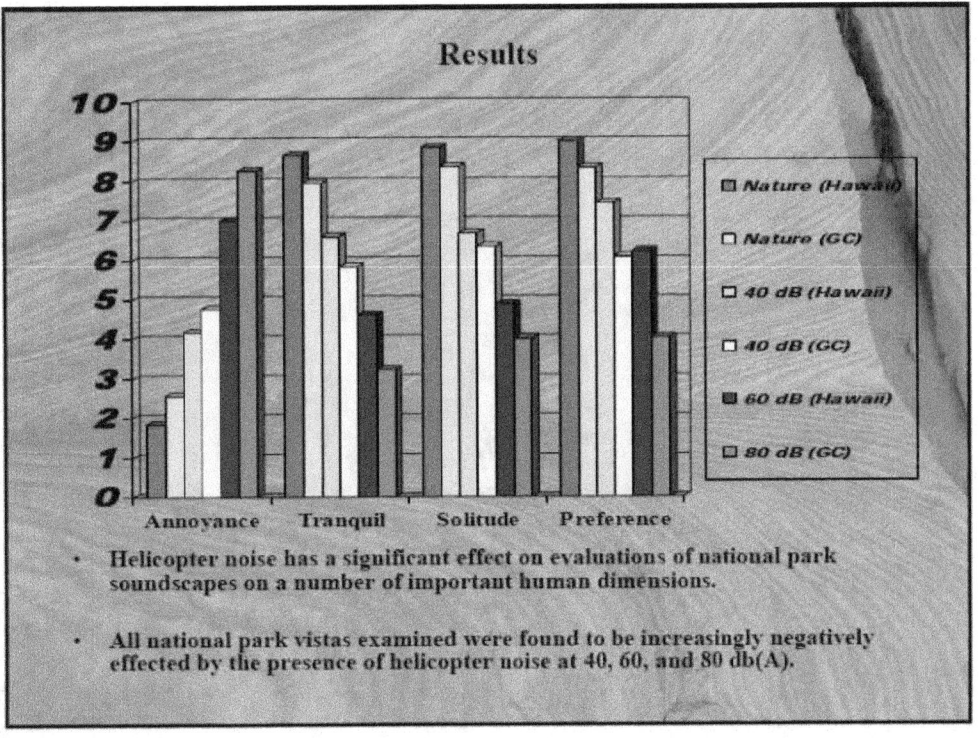

Results

- Helicopter noise has a significant effect on evaluations of national park soundscapes on a number of important human dimensions.

- All national park vistas examined were found to be increasingly negatively effected by the presence of helicopter noise at 40, 60, and 80 db(A).

Source Attribution of Helicopter Noise

- Between Subjects Design: 50 Ss per condition
  - Control (Ambient Nature Sounds)
  - Helicopter Tour Flight
  - NPS Rescue Flight; Maintenance Flight; Firefighting Flight
  - Endangered Species Reintroduction Flight

- Significant effect for helicopter noise using MANOVA.
  - Strongest effects for annoyance, solitude, tranquility, and preference.
  - No significant differences between noise source conditions.
    - Attribution of the noise source is not as important as the mere presence of helicopter noise.

- Mace, B. L., Bell, P. A., Loomis, R. J., & Haas, G. (2003). Source attribution of helicopter noise and associated psychological effects in pristine natural environments. *Journal of Park and Recreation Administration, 21(3), 97-119*

Bryce Canyon National Park
Visitor Studies 2000-01 and 2004-05

- Each year ~200 visitors to one of three lookouts completed a 26-item survey examining visitor motives and experience.
  - 71.6% of the visitors noticed aircraft overflights
  - 55% were bothered or annoyed
  - 25% felt the number of overflights was excessive
  - Quiet technology and reducing the number of flights were the most preferred mitigation alternatives.

  - Helicopters were the type of aircraft noticed most often (47%)
    - commercial jets (36%)
    - single-engine planes (18%)

  - Top two reasons for visiting Bryce each year:
    - View the Natural Scenery (4.89)
    - Enjoy the Natural Soundscape (4.34)

- Zion National Park Transportation System Survey 2001-2005
  - Enjoying the natural soundscape was the 2nd most important reason for visiting Zion.

Current Soundscape Research in Bryce Canyon

- Acoustic zones

- Attended audibility logging

- Sound recording

- Examine different sounds from each acoustic zone in the lab

- Visitor surveying

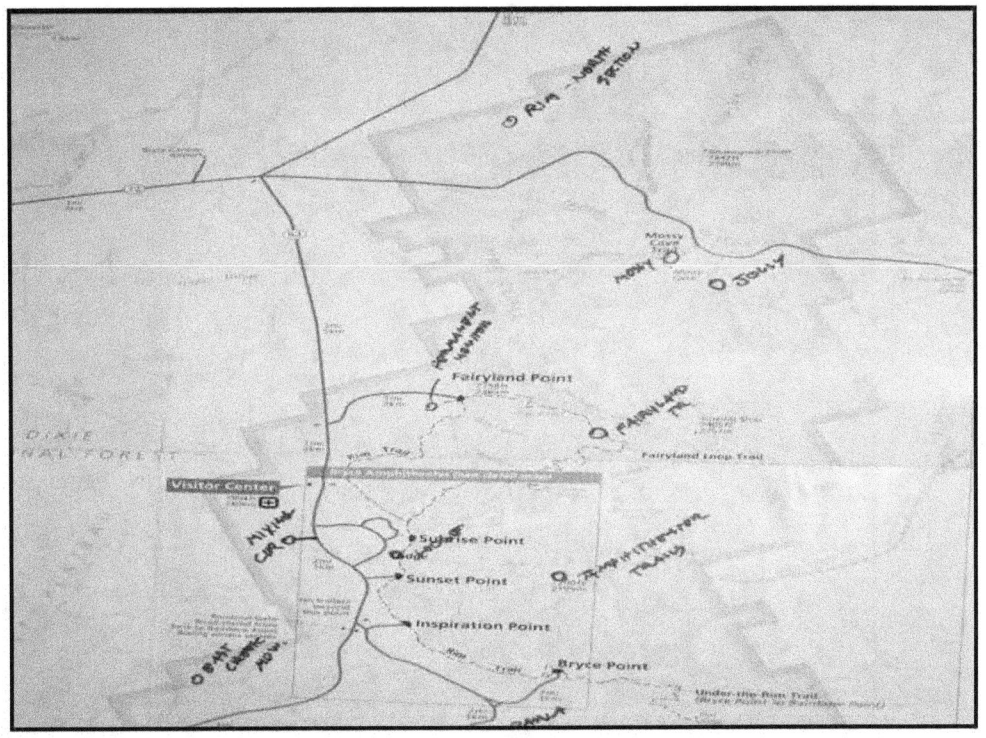

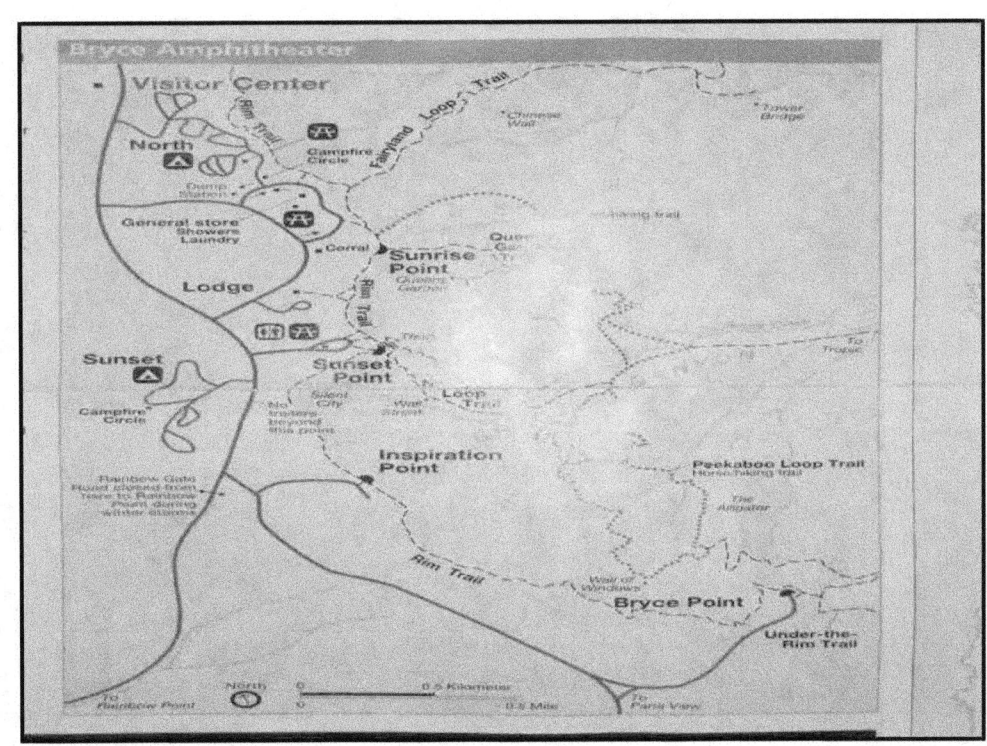

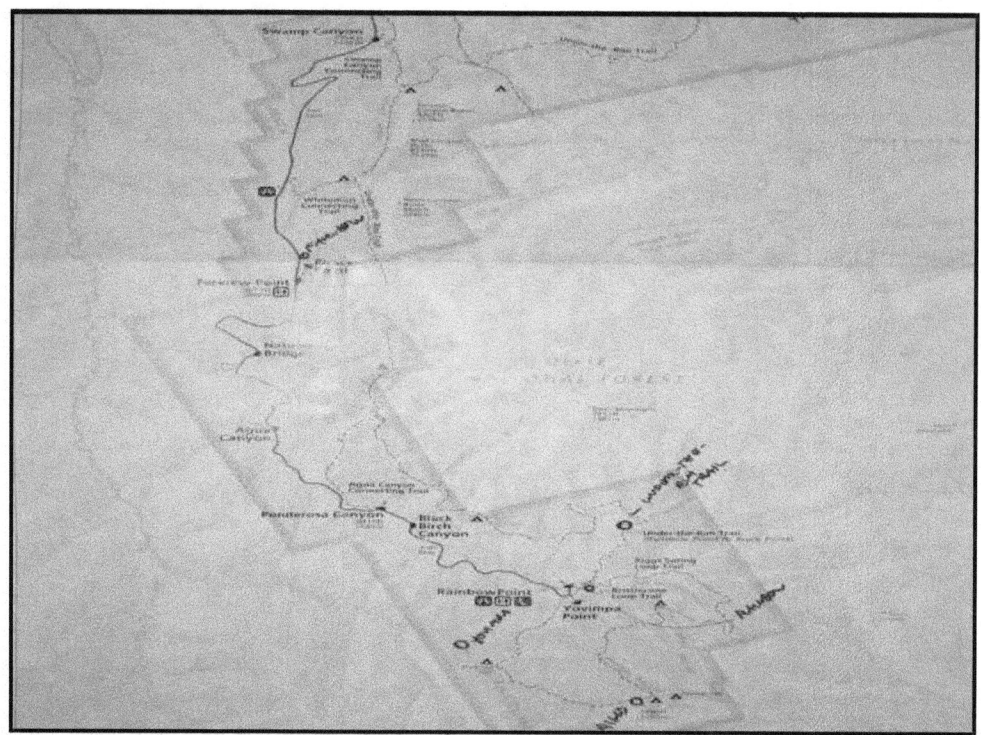

Future Research Directions

- Examine specific dose/response relationships in the lab by expanding the response scales to include wilderness values

  – Laboratory research on jet airplane noise

    - employ landscape evaluation methodology in a controlled setting

    - vary the percent time audible, Leq, Lmax, number of encounters. For example, what happens to the dependent measures when pta drops/increases by 10%, 20%, etc?

    - scaling of wilderness values and other relevant variables to move beyond annoyance and develop thresholds

    - This could be a long-term program of research, costing approx. $150-200,000 for the first 2-3 years.

Future Research Directions

- Lab research should also be conducted to examine different management zones related to soundscapes (acoustic zones).

  – For example, put subjects in the role of a visitor to GCNP in the backcountry wilderness, non-wilderness frontcountry, or a developed zone context.

  – Subjects rate vistas from these parks/sites with different types of sound (including aircraft noise).

  – Data would speak to sound/noise impacts based on management zone and begin to quantitatively address the severity of impact (negligible, minor, major, etc).

  – Costs for this type of study would be $75-$100,000

Future Research Directions

- Identify acoustic zones in a park and collect sound recordings and attended logging data from these zones, followed by, or (ideally) in combination with visitor surveying.

  – Parks affected by overflights, completing ATMP's or soundscape management plans would benefit from this approach.

  – Cost is estimated at $100,000 for each park, depending on number of sites, sampling periods, and travel.

  – Visitor surveys should include demographic, expectation, wilderness value, appropriateness and other questions relevant to the park soundscape.

  – Pre/post airport field opportunity in Zion using the approach currently being employed in Bryce.

- Observational methods — visitor tracking at viewpoints in parks affected by aircraft overflights

  – Cost is estimated at $75,000-$100,000 initially, including pilot testing, instrument development, and a set of data at one park. Costs would decrease if the same protocol was used at other parks.

How can the value of the wilderness experience be defined and measured?

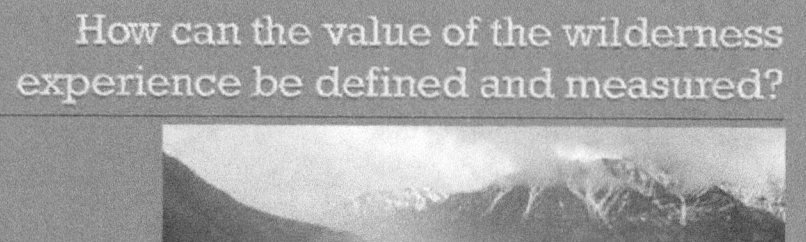

Bill Borrie
Professor,
College of Forestry and Conservation
University of Montana, Missoula.

Limitations of single-item measures

Such as:

Visitor satisfaction, enjoyment,
acceptability, annoyance, etc.

Inadequate cognitive
ability to process

W.T. Borrie, J.W. Roggenbuck and R.B. Hall, 1998. The problem of verbal reports in recreation research: review recommendations, and new directions, Tourism Analysis 2 , pp. 175–183

Post-hoc vs. in-situ
Strategic responding
Where do expectations
come from?

• which context

• which experience

Borrie, W.T., and R.M. Birzell. 2001. Approaches to measuring quality of the wilderness experience. Pages 29-38 in Visitor Use Density and Wilderness Experience: Proceedings (W.A. Friedmund and D.N. Cole, compilers). USDA Forest Service Rocky Mountain Research Station RMRS-P-20, Fort Collins, CO.

Limits of Acceptable Change

Standard approach to acceptability
Identify   to be preserved
  · Visitor experience objectives, such as solitude
Develop   that measure qualities
  · based on clear criteria of good indicator
Set   for those indicators
  · based on what is considered <u>acceptable</u>
  · chosen by public, or normative standards

⦿Important to document link between
              / factors of influence and
qualities
      ⦿   physical, social,
  and managerial conditions

McCool, S.F., Cole, D.W., 1997.
Proceedings—Limits of Acceptable Change
and Related Planning Processes: Progress
and Future Directions. General Technical
Report INT-GTR-371, US Forest Service,
Washington, DC.

Qualities of good indicators

Selection of indicators should be
based on
  · not just what we know how to measure
  · not just what is most cost effective

Which criteria are
  · Most
    · According to visitors
  · Most   / best proxy
  · Most   (to factors of influence)

Watson, A., Glaspell, B., Christensen, N., Lachapelle, P.,
Sahanatien, V., and Gertsch, F. (2007). Giving Voice to
Wildlands Visitors: Selecting Indicators to Protect and Sustain
Experiences in the Eastern Arctic of Nunavut. *Environmental
Management*, 40(6), p. 880-8.

Need for multi-phase, multi-method approach

Experiences are dynamic, emergent, and not prescribed / goal-directed
- the meanings, narratives, & values

approach to document which qualities are most important / influential

approach to consider data
- underlying structure (factor analyses)
- relationship to conditions / factors of influence

What qualities?

Davenport, M.A., W.T. Borrie, W.A. Freimund, and R.E. Manning. 2002. Assessing the relationship between desired experiences and support for management actions at Yellowstone National Park using multiple methods. Journal of Park and Recreation Administration 20, 3, 51 - 64

- opportunity to see abundant & diverse wildlife
- natural scenery
- see & learn about rare, natural objects

Patterson, M.E., A.E. Watson, D.R. Williams, and J.R. Roggenbuck. 1998. An hermeneutic approach to studying the nature of wilderness experiences. Journal of Leisure Research 30, 4, 423-452

- having to make independent decisions
- challenge

Glaspell B., A. Watson, K. Kneeshaw and D. Pendergrast. 2003. Selecting Indicators and Understanding Their Role in Wilderness Experience Stewardship at Gates of the Arctic National Park and Preserve. George Wright Forum 20(3): 59-71.

- freedom from rules & regulations
- untrammeled wildlife
- challenge of access
- risk & uncertainty

·Watson, A., Glaspell, B., Christensen, N., Lachapelle, P., Sahanatien, V., and Gertsch, F. (2007). Giving Voice to Wildlands Visitors: Selecting Indicators to Protect and Sustain Experiences in the Eastern Arctic of Nunavut. Environmental Management, 46(6), p. 880-8.

- challenge & accomplishment
- connection with nature
- learning & appreciation
- isolation in nature (quiet, far from civilization)

Public Law 88-577 - Wilderness Act

Sec. 2(c) A wilderness, in contrast with those areas where man and his own works dominate the landscape, is hereby recognized as an area where the earth and its community of life are untrammeled by man, where man himself is a visitor who does not remain.

Trammel:

1: a net for catching birds or fish

2: an adjustable pothook for a fireplace crane

3: **a shackle used for making a horse amble**

4: **something impeding activity, progress, or freedom : restraint**

Merriam-Webster Online Dictionary

Public Law 88-577 - Wilderness Act

An area of wilderness is further defined to mean in this Act an area of undeveloped Federal land retaining , without permanent improvements or human habitation, which is protected and managed so as to preserve its natural conditions and which

(1) generally appears to have been affected primarily by the forces of nature, with the ;

(2) has outstanding opportunities for ;

(3) has at least five thousand acres of land or is of sufficient size as to make practicable its preservation and use in an unimpaired condition; and

(4) may also contain ecological, geological, or other features of scientific, educational, scenic, or historical value.

Public Law 93-622 – The so-called Eastern Wilderness Areas Act enacted on January 3, 1975
Sec. 2(b) Therefore, the Congress finds and declares that is in the national interest that these and similar areas in the eastern half of the United States be promptly designated as wilderness within the National Wilderness Preservation System, in order to preserve such areas as an enduring resource of wilderness which shall be managed to promote and perpetuate the wilderness character of the land and its specific values of

,

,

scientific study,

,

and

Summary of wilderness character:

Primeval character & influence
- Imprint of human work substantially unnoticeable
- Counter to modern civilization:
  - Expanding settlement
  - Mechanization

Untrammeled
Natural condition
Solitude
Primitive and unconfined recreation
Physical and mental challenge
Inspiration

Landres, P., C. Barns, J.G. Dennis, T. Devine, P. Geissler, C.S. McCasland, L. Merigliano, J. Seastrand, and R. Swain. 2008. Keeping it Wild: An Interagency Strategy to Monitor Trends in Wilderness Character Across the National Wilderness Preservation System. 81 pages. USDA Forest Service, Rocky Mountain Research Station General Technical Report RMRS-GTR-212, Fort Collins, CO.

Research needs & project costs

Need for in-situ, multi-method approach
- Examining how parks are perceived and experienced by visitors
  - What values & meanings are most important?
    - Fundamentally underlies attitudes towards management actions, experience motivations, and expectations
    - Relationship of natural sounds to other aspects of experience of parks
    - development of proxy indicators for qualities
  - What conditions have direct influence on qualities?
    - Grau & Priemund found that natural soundscapes are not independent of other setting attributes

Need for validation across different parks
- Validation of data structure, proxies, and factors of influence
- Generalizability of qualities, indicators
- Approx. $85,000 per park.
- Tanner, et al. (2008) examined four parks
  - Tanner, R.J., W.A. Freimund, W.T. Borrie, and R.N. Moisey. 2008. A Meta-study of the Values of Visitors to Four Protected Areas in the Western United States. Leisure Sciences, 30, 1-14.

Public process for development of standards

The National Park Service Organic Act
Aug. 25, 1916

The service thus established shall promote and regulate the use of the Federal areas known as national parks, monuments, and reservations hereinafter specified by such means and measures as conform to the fundamental purpose of the said parks, monuments, and reservations, which purpose is to conserve the and the
and the
therein and to provide for the in such manner and by such means as will leave them unimpaired for the enjoyment of future generations.

Scenary

Beauty, aesthetics
Pastoral
- gentle, harmonious relationship with humans

Romantic / transcendentalist
- calming, peaceful, reflective
- restorative, refreshing, rejuvenating
- a sanctuary, sacred space, spiritual closeness

Natural and historic objects

Our national heritage
- symbolic

unique,
'must – see" features
monumentalism
- big, sublime landscapes

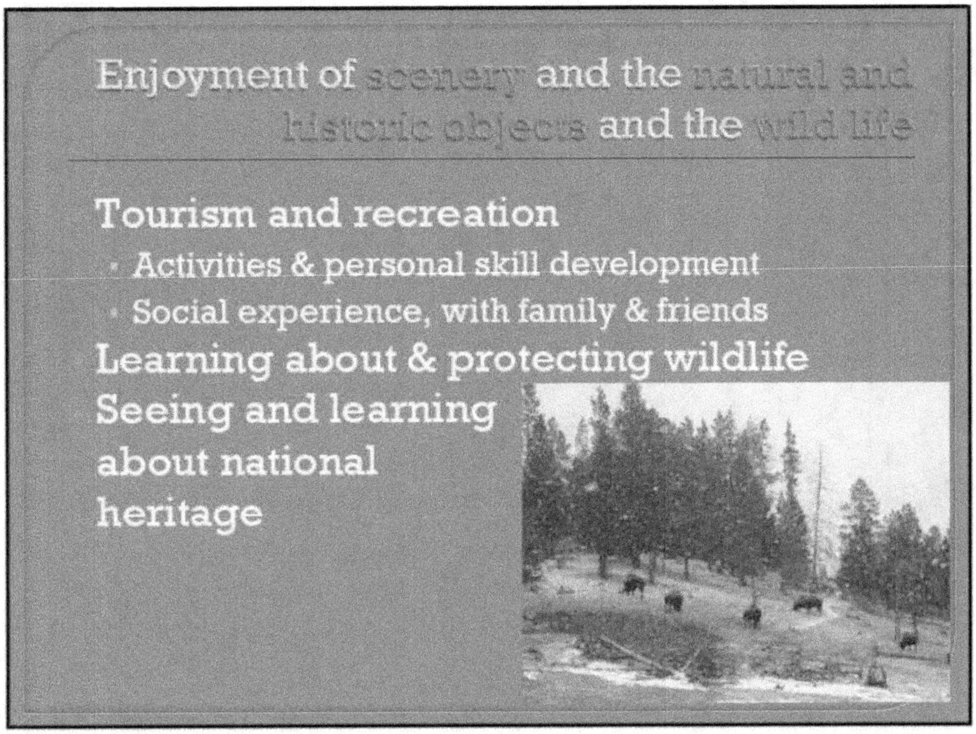
Enjoyment of scenery and the natural and historic objects and the wild life
Tourism and recreation
Activities & personal skill development
Social experience, with family & friends
Learning about & protecting wildlife
Seeing and learning about national heritage

Data Gaps
in
Dose-Response Work

Nicholas P. Miller

Harris Miller Miller & Hanson Inc.

National Parks and Visitor Response to Sounds
Data Gaps

- **Other Sources – Cost ~$500k / source-park**
  - Snow-machines
  - Personal watercraft
  - High altitude jets
  - Traffic – distant or close-by?

National Parks and Visitor Response to Sounds
Data Gaps

www.hmmh.com

- **Auditory / Experiential Comparison w/ Metrics ~$300k??**
  - Organized listening for decision-makers
    - Listen then write
    - Write while listening
    - Logging
  - Several locations w/ different management objectives
  - Simultaneous monitoring and observer logging
  - Post-listening debriefing
  - Comparison w/ range of metrics
  - "Let the resource speak for itself"

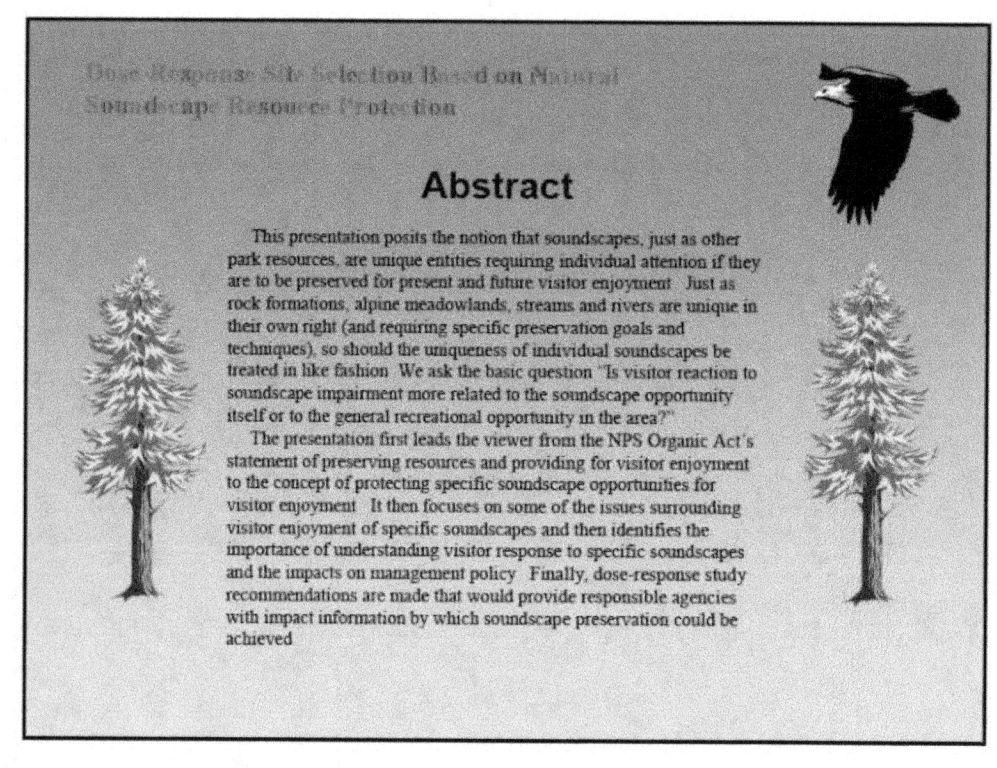

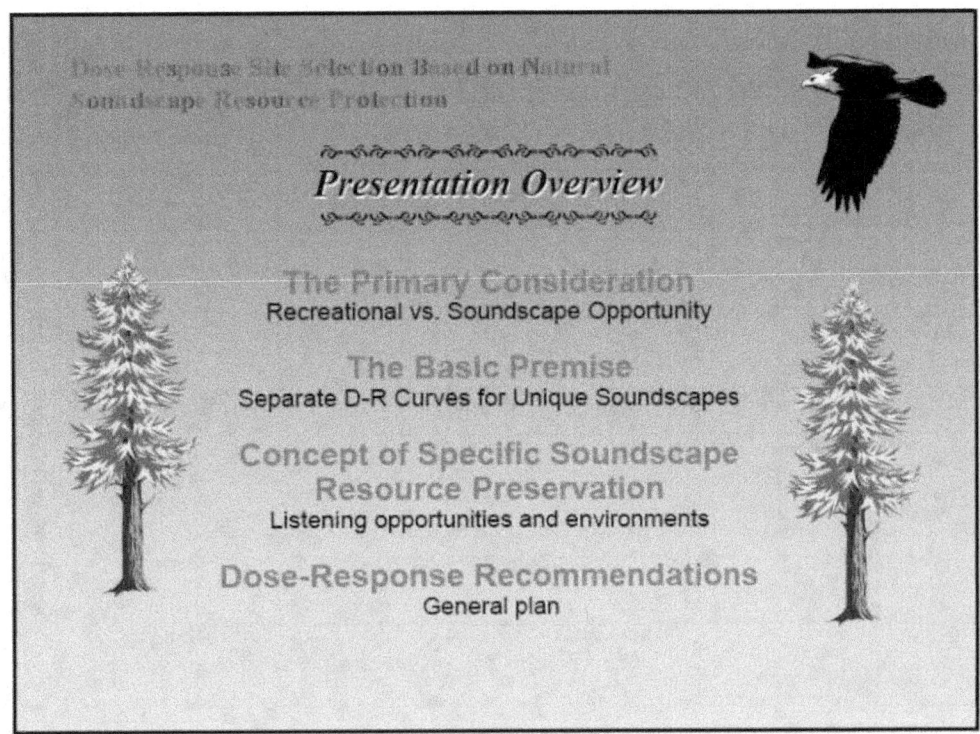

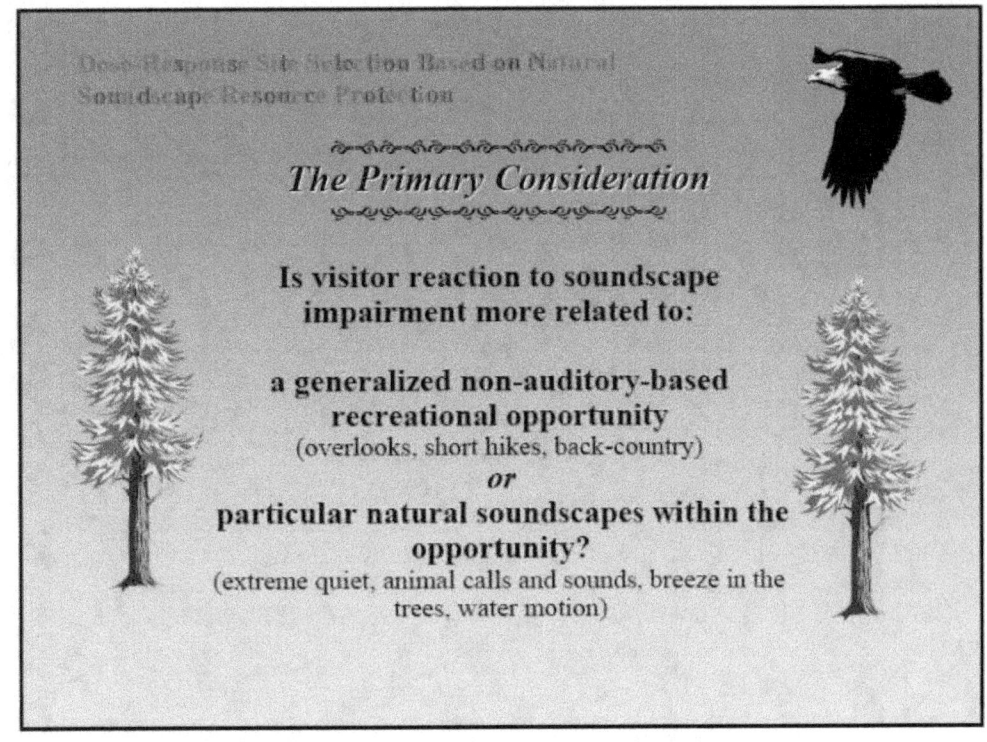

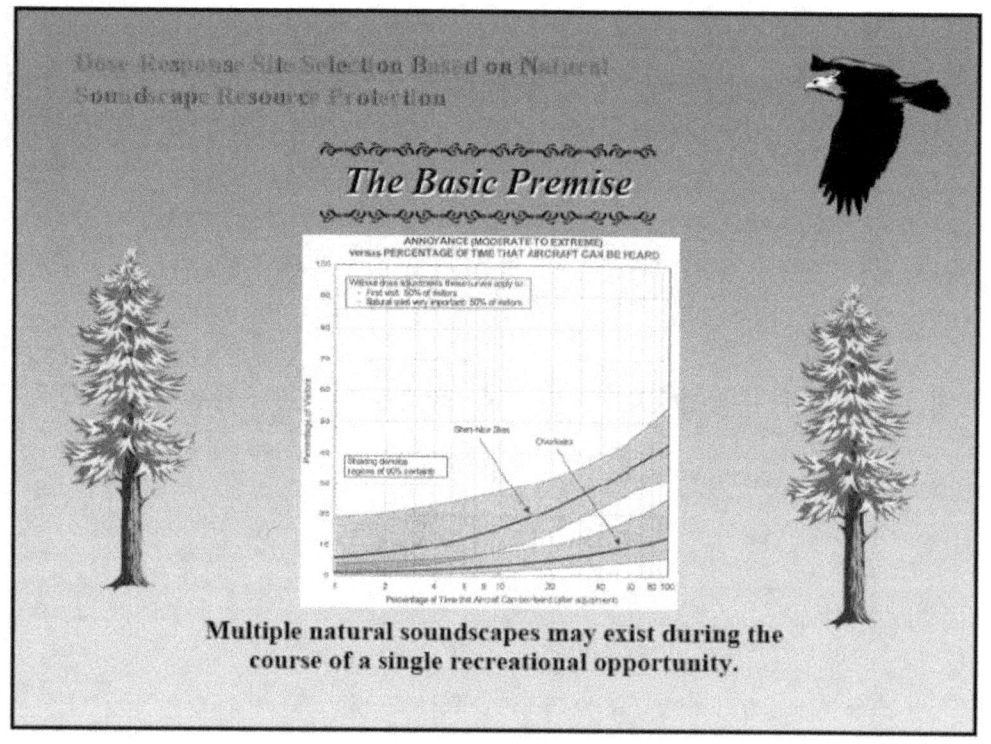

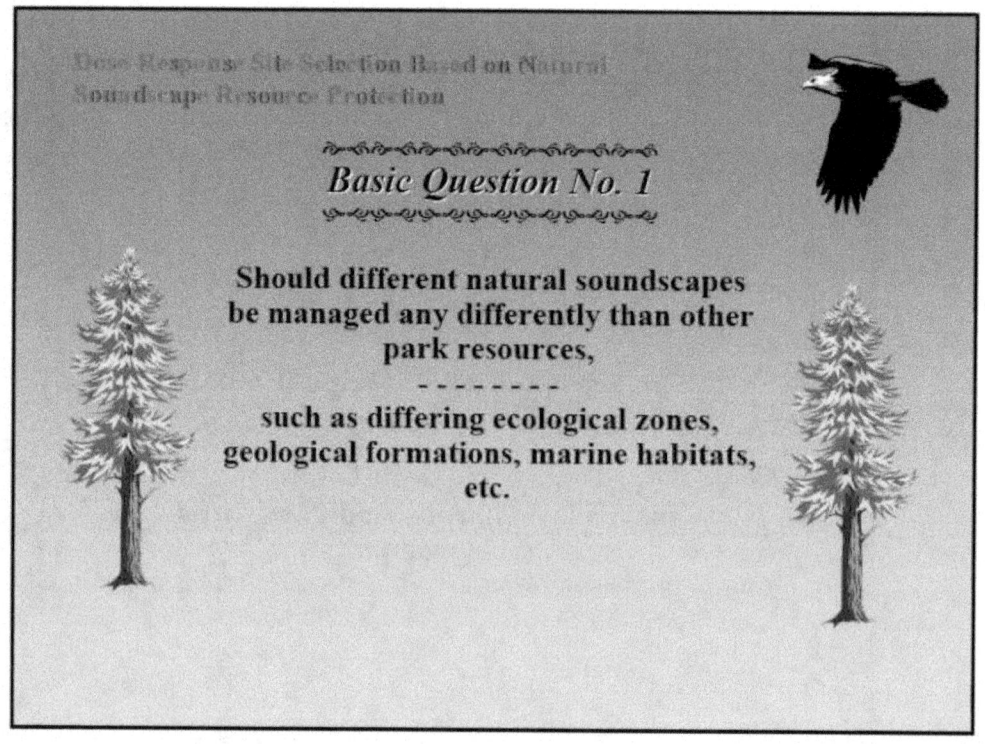

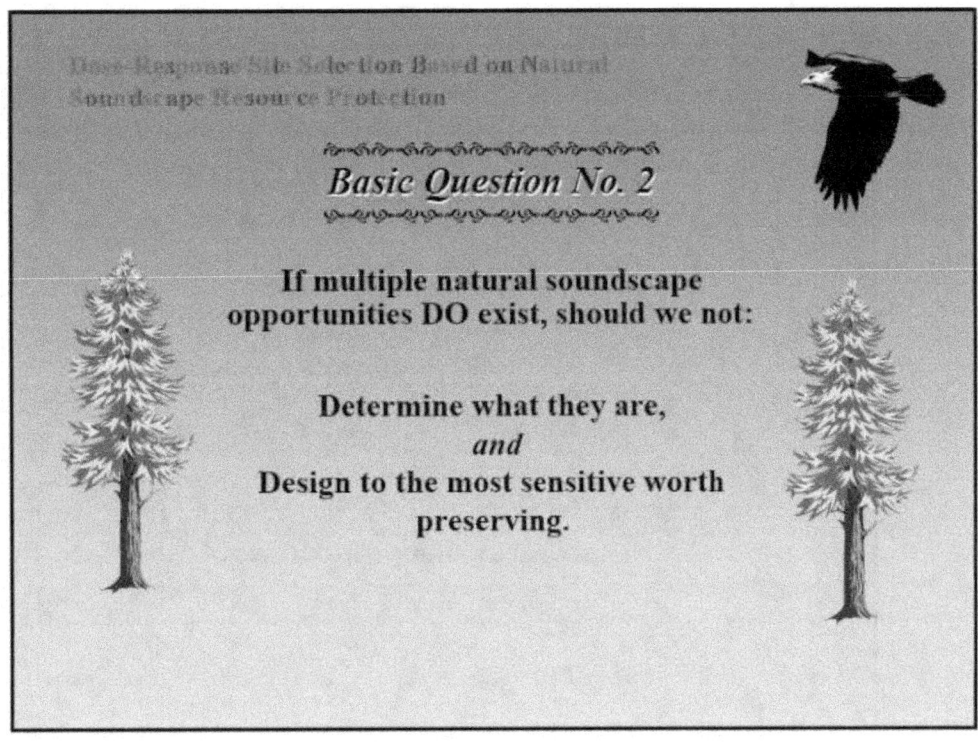

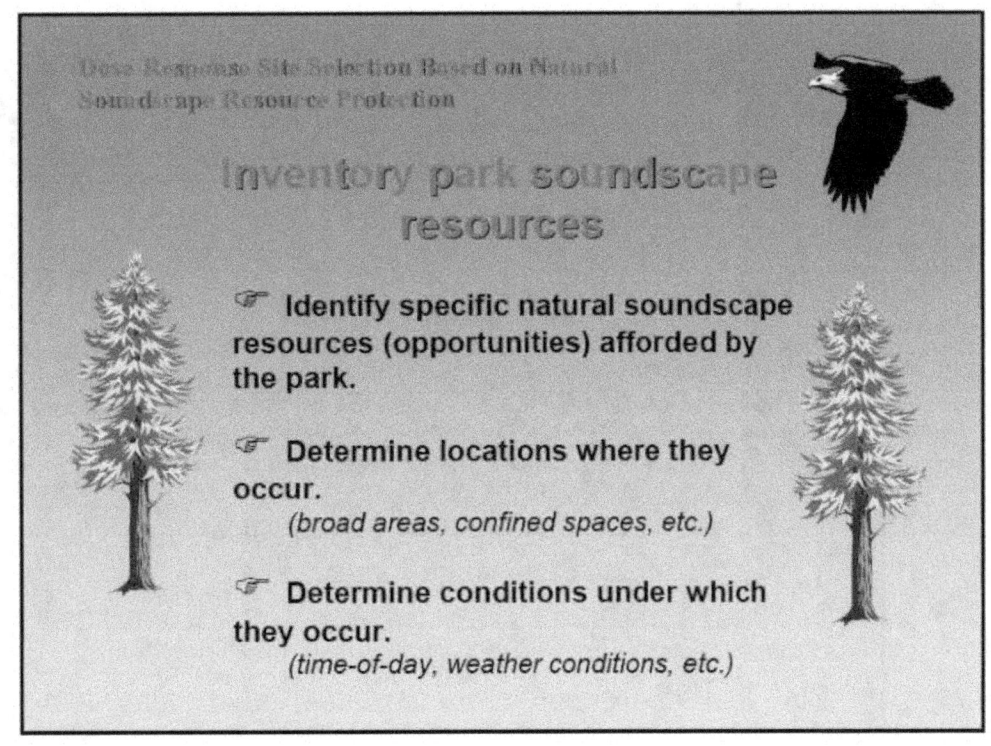

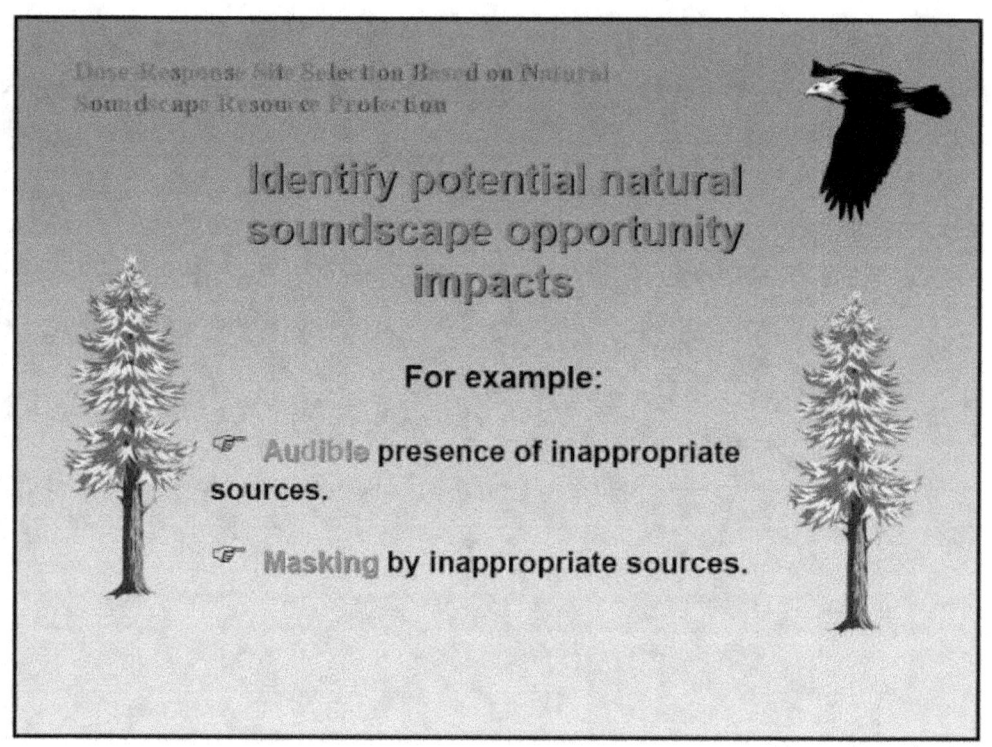

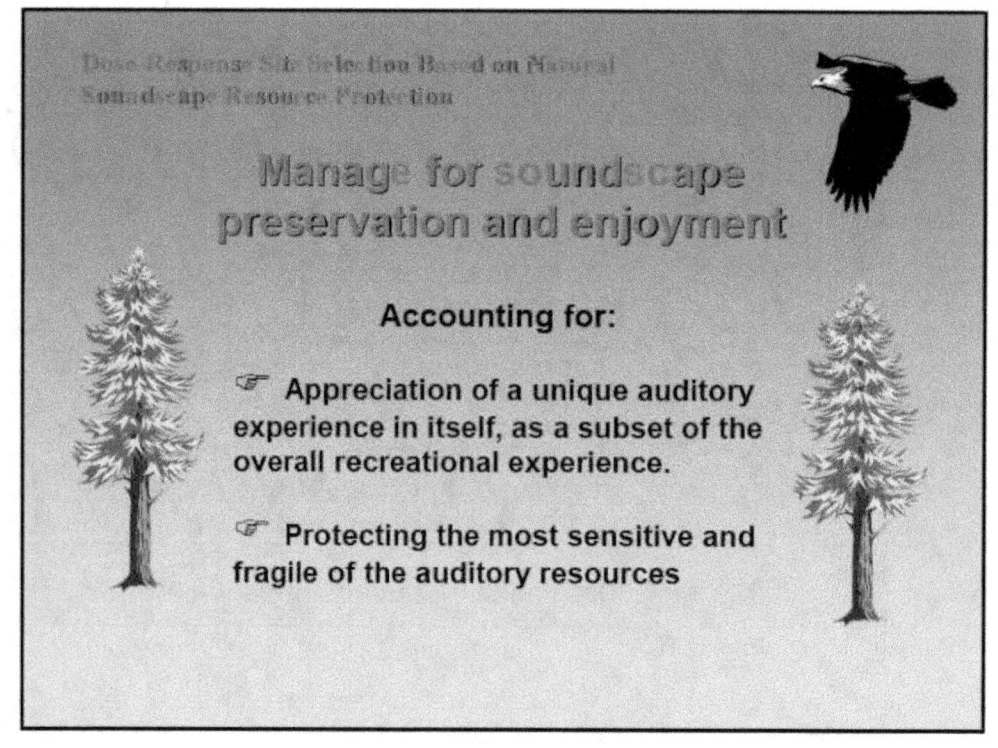

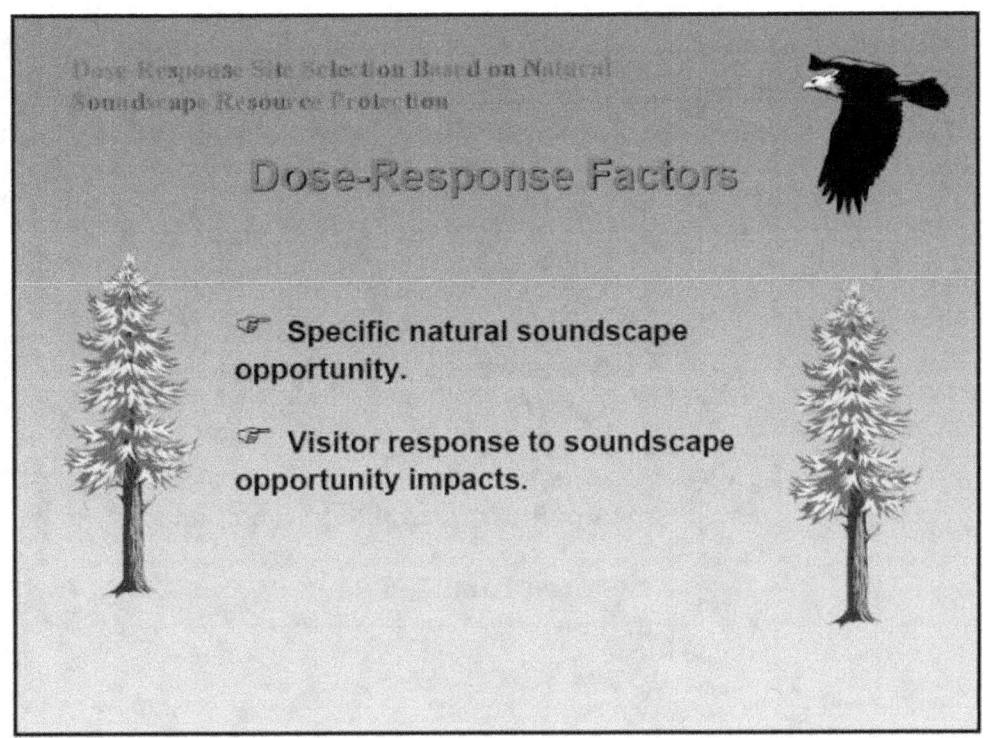

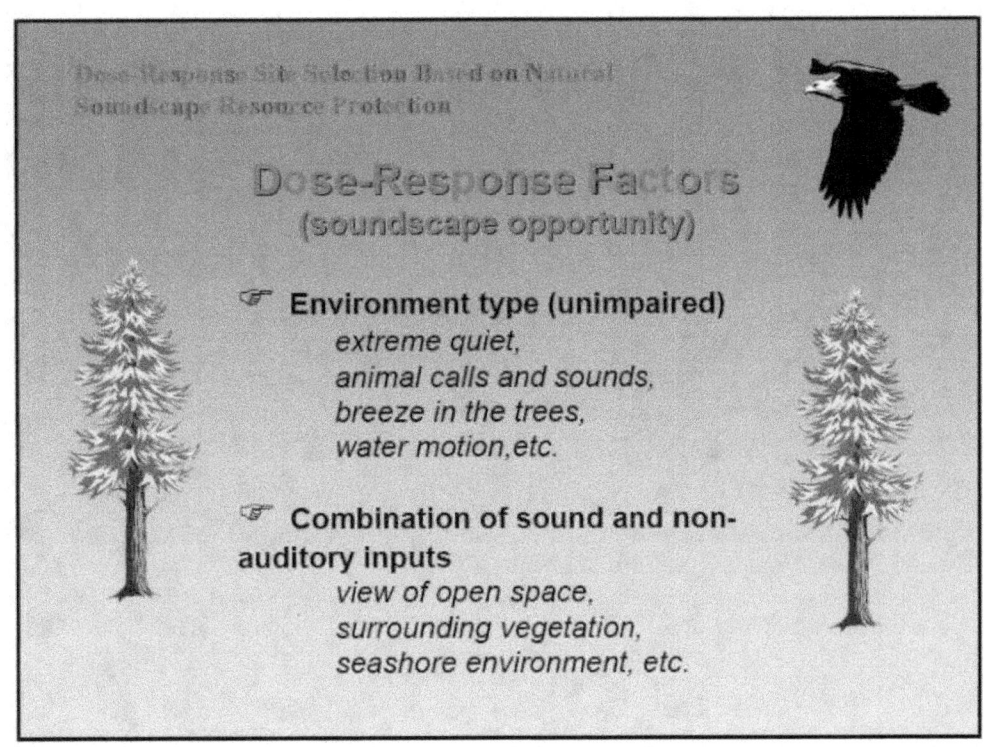

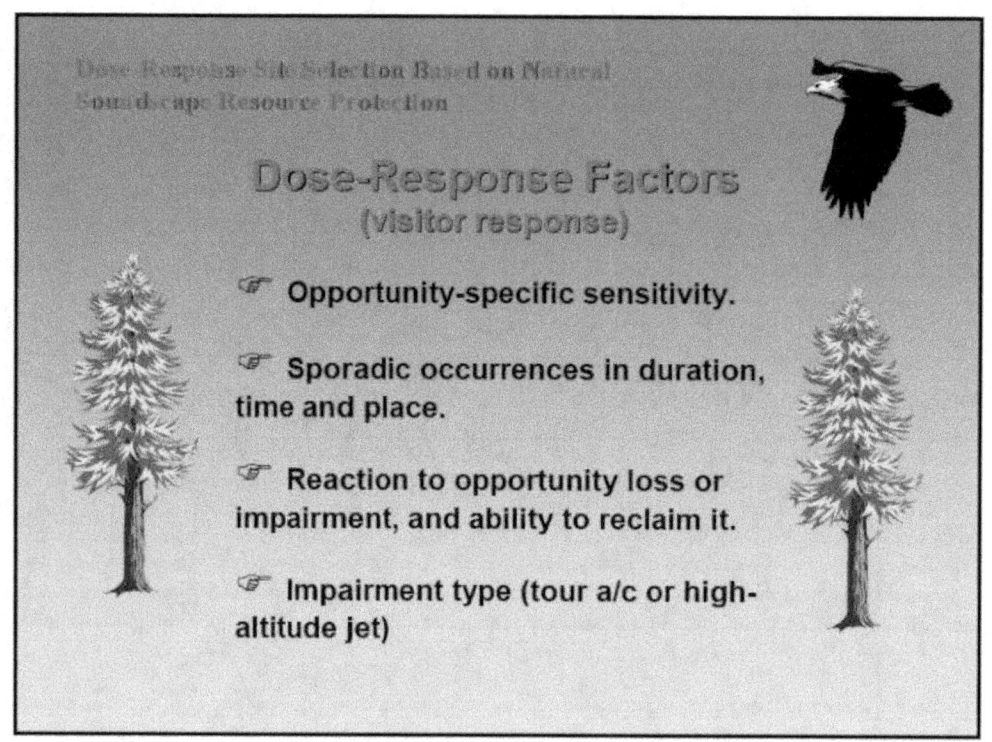

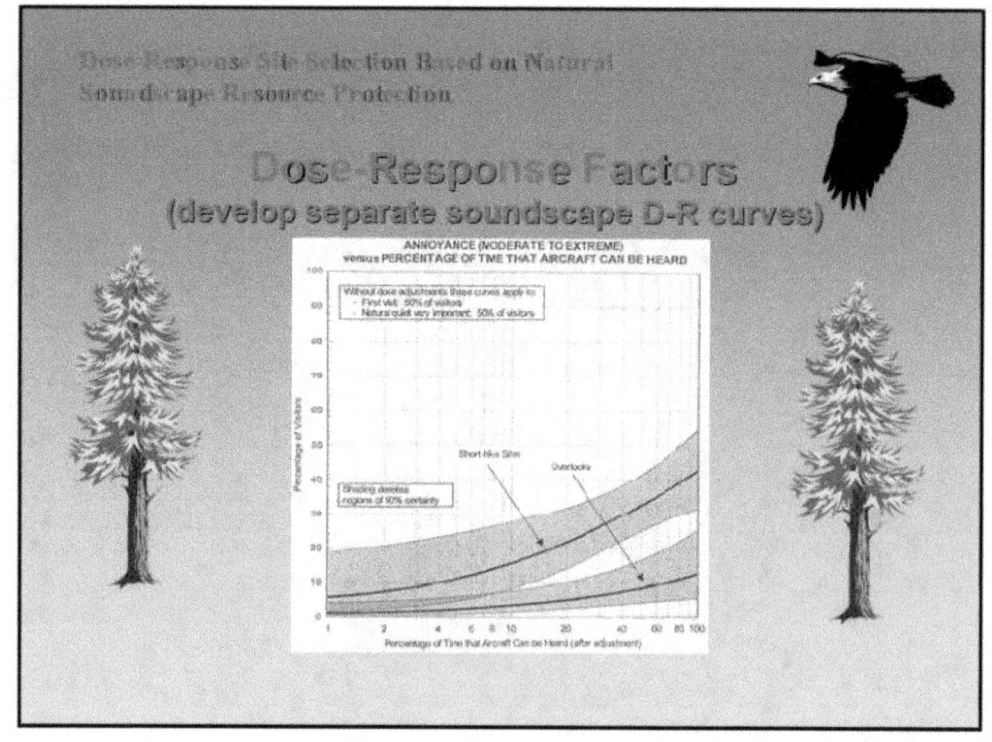

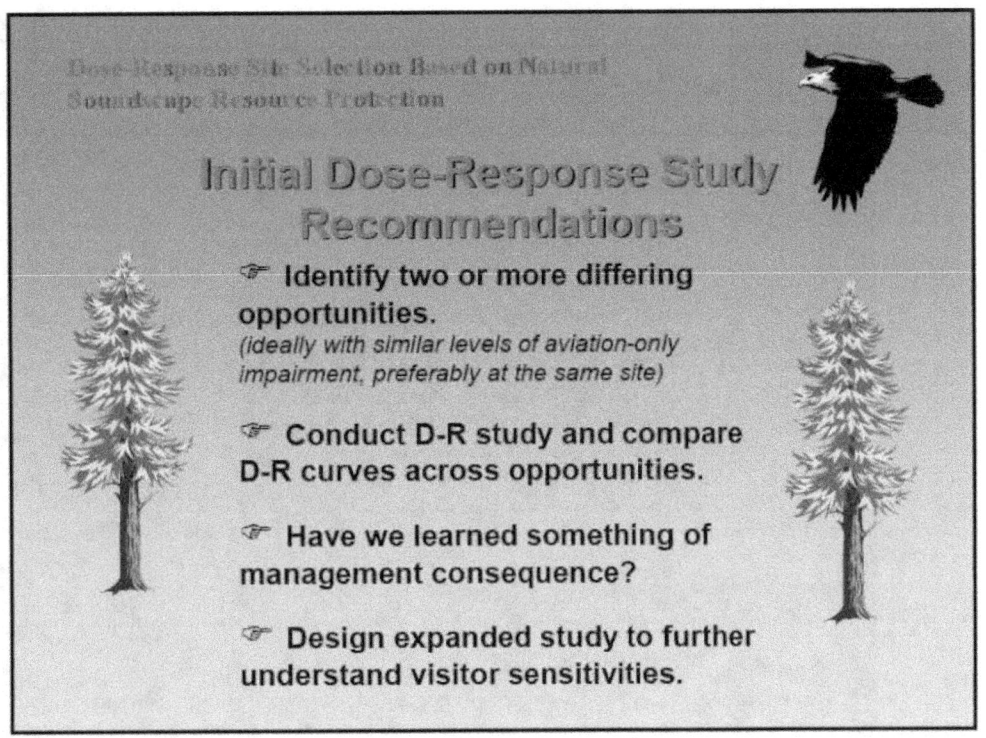

Major Data Gaps: How Can They Be Resolved?

Human Response to Aviation Noise in Protected Natural Areas
28-29 October 2008

Grant Anderson

Overview

- Major data gaps:
  - Backcountry activities
  - Each visitor: Different doses/responses over several-week period
- How resolved?
  - Hiker location/activity: Hour by hour
  - Hiker responses: Sufficiently thorough
  - Hiker doses: Sufficiently precise
- Proposed implementation

.... all preliminary ideas, needing much more thought

Presentation 2.3 - Anderson

Major Data Gaps

- Backcountry activities:
  - No dose-response (DR) data
  - Extensive land area
- Each hiker in backcountry:
  - Different doses from day/day, hour/hour
  - Different locations/activities:
    - On the trail, by the lake, at a campsite, at an overlook
    - Hiking, camping, relaxing, enjoying, eating, sleeping
    - For all of these:
      - Does DR relation depends upon activity?
      - If yes: Major statistical strength in analysis

Human Response to Aviation Noise in Protected Natural Areas: 28 October 2008 · Slide 2 · Major data gaps: How can they be resolved? Grant Anderson

How Resolved?
Hour-by-hour Hiker Location/Activity

- Attach GPS "track stick" to backpack

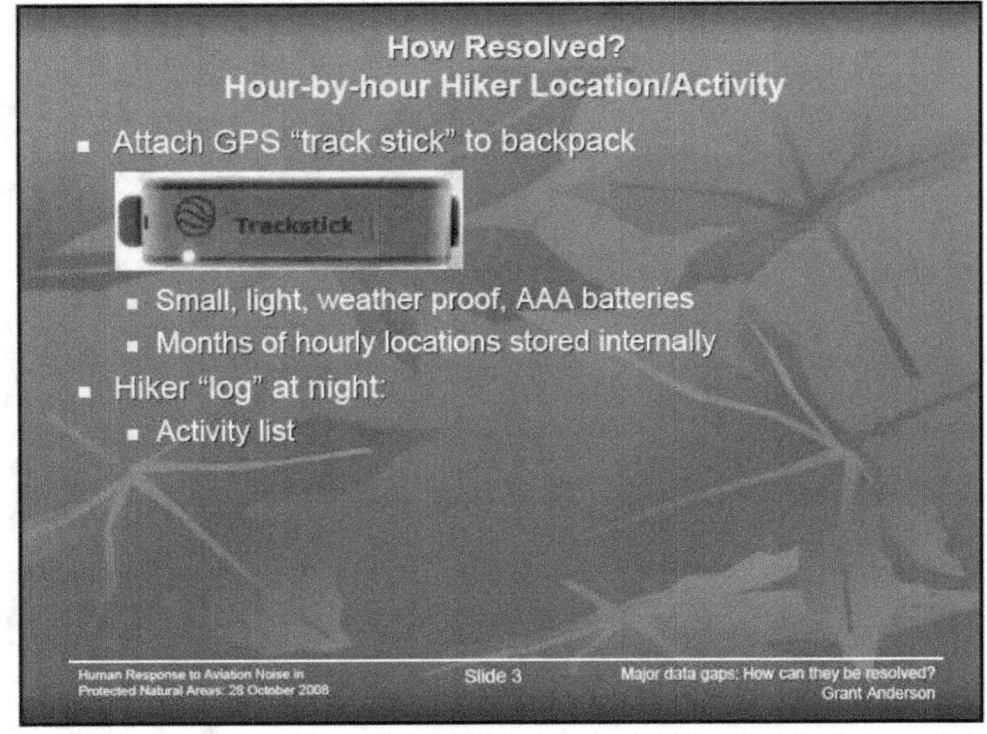

  - Small, light, weather proof, AAA batteries
  - Months of hourly locations stored internally
- Hiker "log" at night:
  - Activity list

Human Response to Aviation Noise in Protected Natural Areas: 28 October 2008 · Slide 3 · Major data gaps: How can they be resolved? Grant Anderson

115

How Resolved?
Sufficiently Thorough Hiker Responses

- Short hiker log/questionnaire at night:
  - Responses for <u>today</u>:
    - Activity by hour
    - When noticed aircraft noise? What were you doing?
    - At that time: 5-point response questions (2 responses)
  - How compares to <u>yesterday</u>?
  - Acknowledge that hiker knows purpose of questionnaire
- Interview at end of hike:
  - Mediator variables
  - Return log/questionnaire and equipment
  - Get significant "reward"

Human Response to Aviation Noise in Protected Natural Areas: 28 October 2008 · Slide 4 · Major data gaps: How can they be resolved? Grant Anderson

How Resolved?
Sufficiently Precise Hiker Doses (<u>Option 1</u>)

- Volpe: Air Traffic Control System Command Center (bound to be useful in this effort)

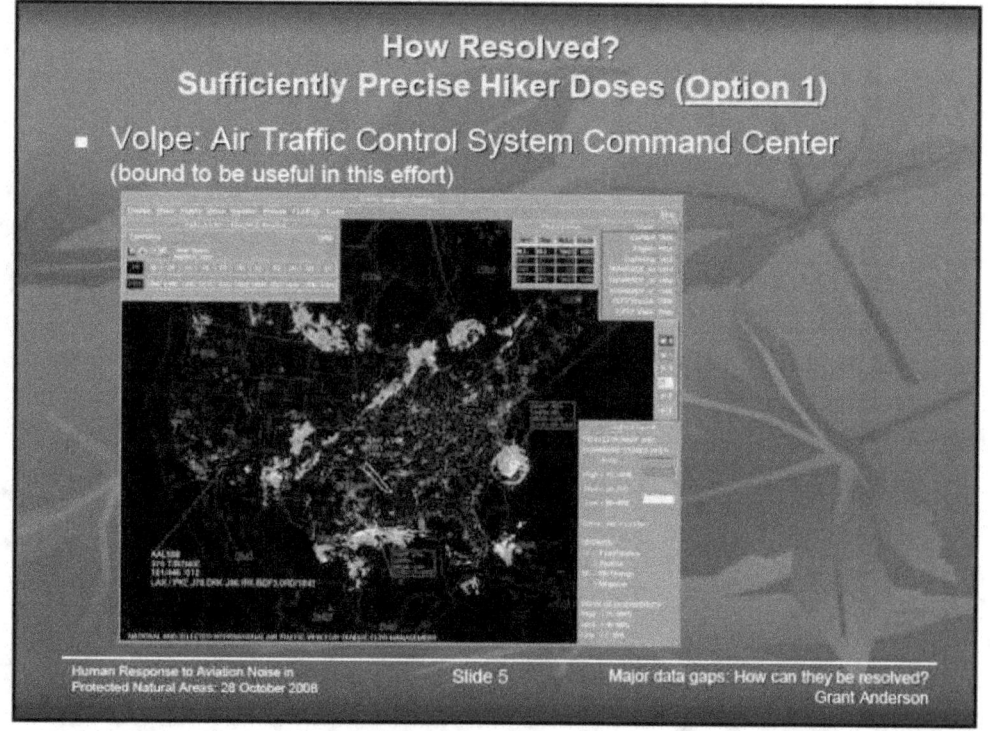

Human Response to Aviation Noise in Protected Natural Areas: 28 October 2008 · Slide 5 · Major data gaps: How can they be resolved? Grant Anderson

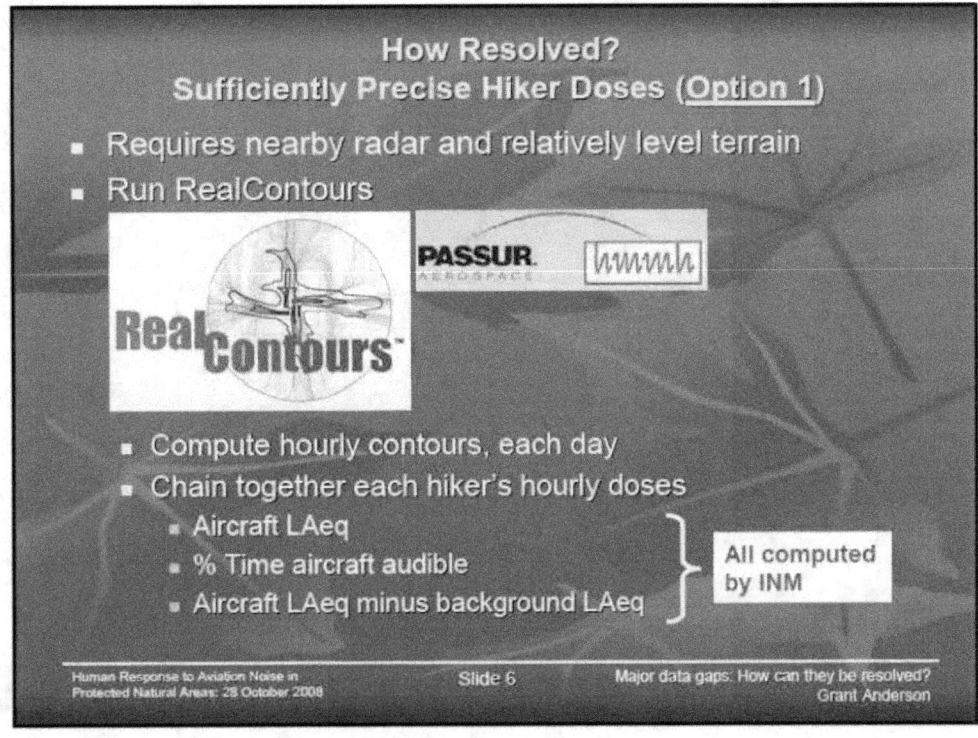

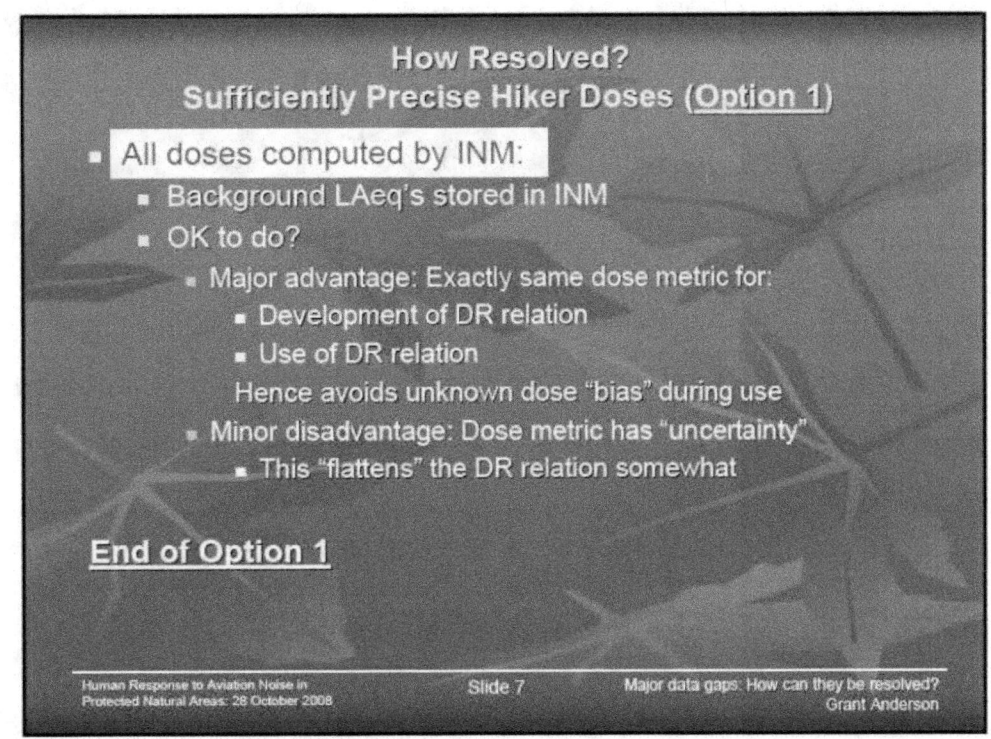

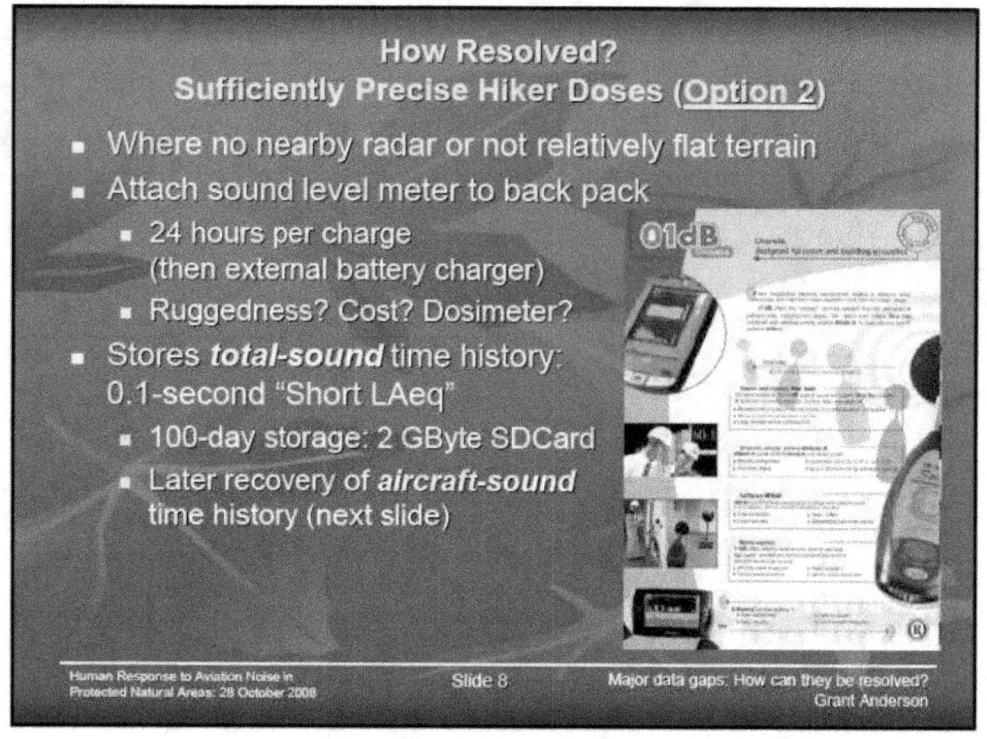

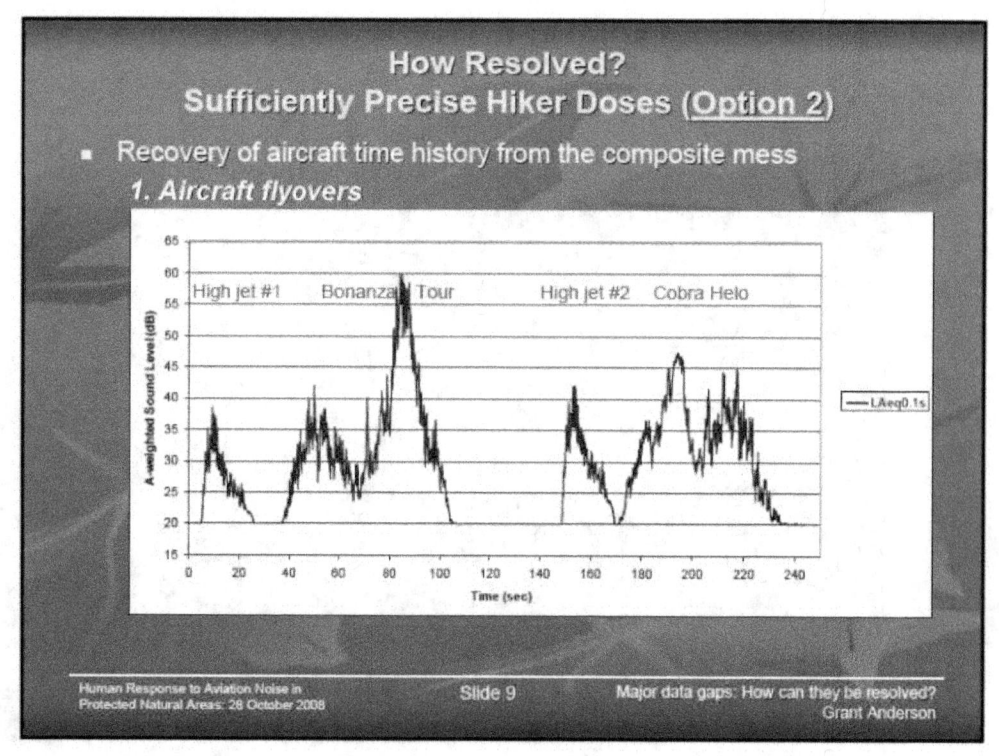

Presentation 2.3 - Anderson

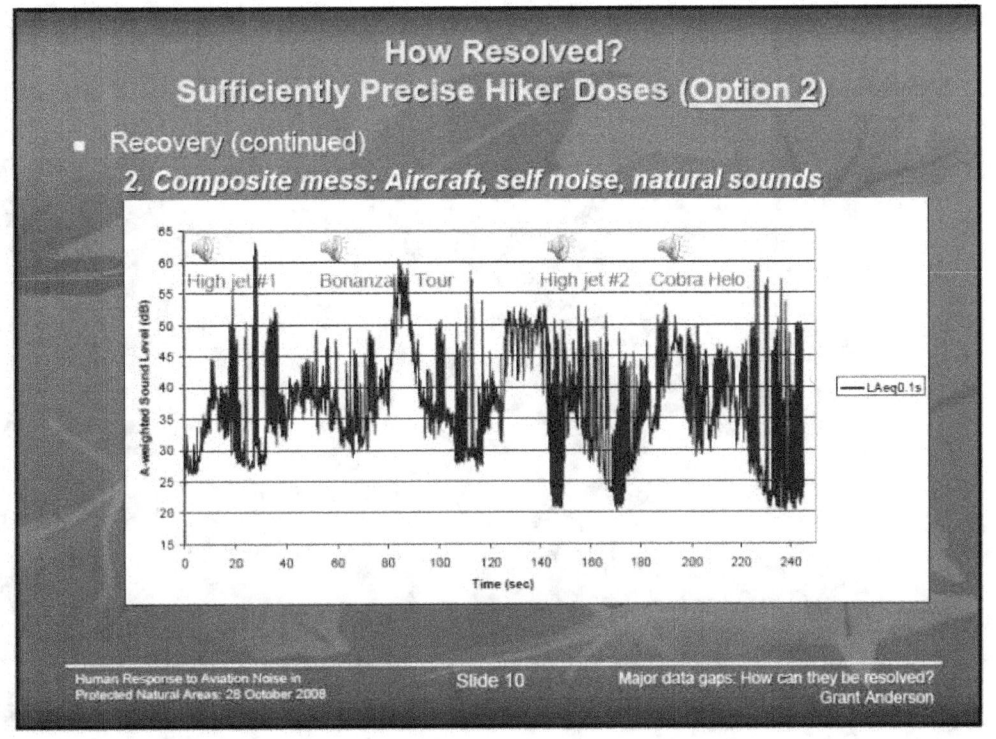

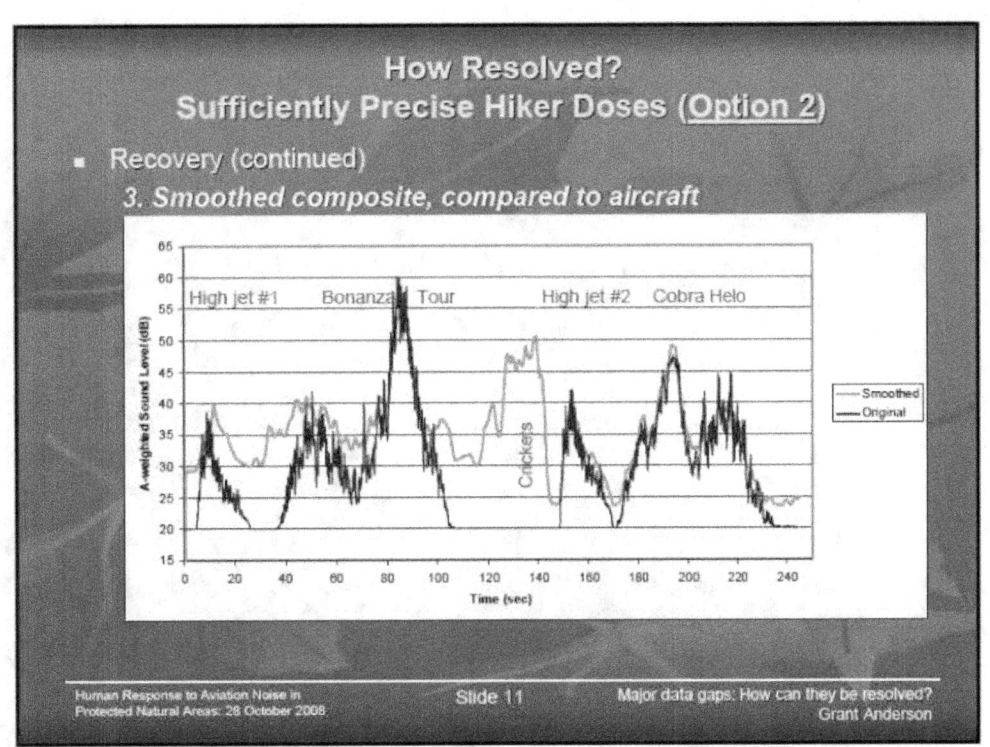

How Resolved?
Sufficiently Precise Hiker Doses (Option 2)

- Recovery (continued)

  4. *SEL comparison*

Aircraft	SELs (dBA)		
	True (T)	Recovered (R)	R minus T
High Jet #1	42	48	+6
Bonanza Tour	64	63	-1
High Jet #2	46	47	+1
Cobra Helo	56	57	+1

End of Option 2

Human Response to Aviation Noise in Protected Natural Areas: 28 October 2008   Slide 12   Major data gaps: How can they be resolved?
Grant Anderson

Proposed Implementation

Determine Backcountry Dose-Response

- Choose parks
- Design entire program thoroughly:
  - Design dose method
  - Design/approve response method
  - Reduce costs/risks (lost/stolen equipment)
  - Many other details
- Undertake the DR measurements (2 weeks at 3 parks?)
- Determine the dose-response relations and their uncertainties

Human Response to Aviation Noise in Protected Natural Areas: 28 October 2008   Slide 13   Major data gaps: How can they be resolved?
Grant Anderson

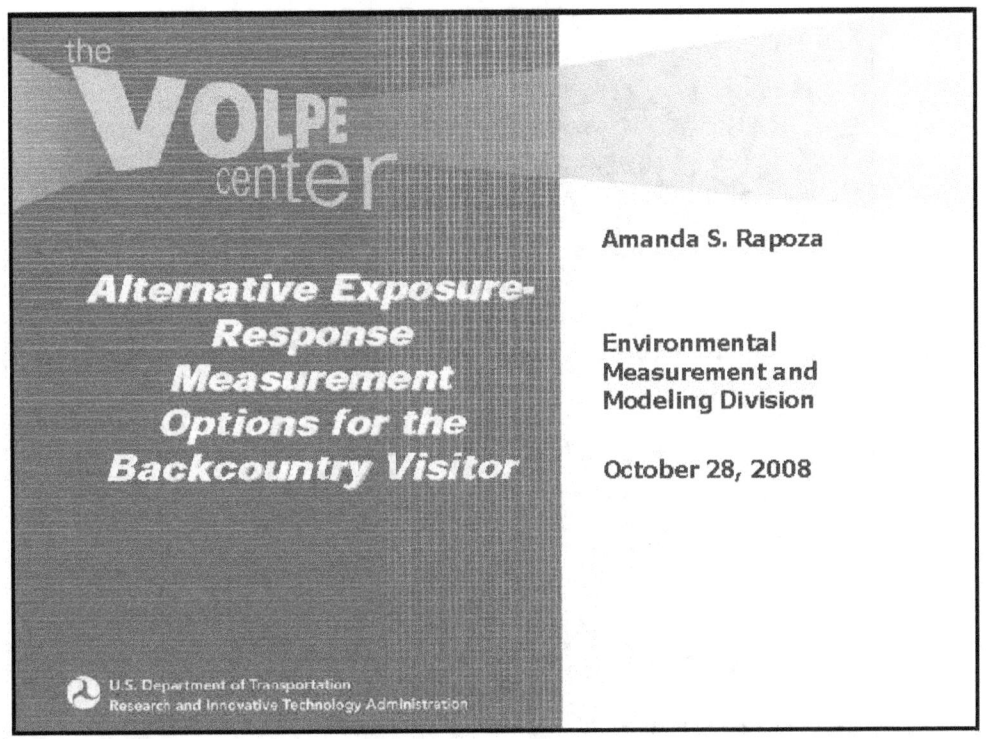

the **VOLPE** center

Alternative Exposure-Response Measurement Options for the Backcountry Visitor

Amanda S. Rapoza

Environmental Measurement and Modeling Division

October 28, 2008

U.S. Department of Transportation
Research and Innovative Technology Administration

Problem: We do not have data to develop exposure-response relationships for visitors to backcountry areas, as this data is logistically difficult and time-consuming to collect

Proposed Solution: Certain characteristics of backcountry visitors may be found in visitors at other locations. Exposure-response relationships using these visitors could serve as a proxy for backcountry exposure-response relationships.

the **VOLPE** center

U.S. Department of Transportation
Research and Innovative Technology Administration

Data Gap

The backcountry visitor

- Low visitation rates + Remote = Large Effort

How can we model these visitor experience impacts?

- Find the characteristics of these visitors.
- Can we replicate these characteristics elsewhere?

VOLPE center

 U.S. Department of Transportation
Research and Innovative Technology Administration

Visitor Characteristics

Attentiveness

- Activity
- Group size
- Presence of children in group
- Crowding

Expectations

- Reason for visit
- Previous visit experience
- Knowledge of overflights

VOLPE center

 U.S. Department of Transportation
Research and Innovative Technology Administration

Visitor Attentiveness: Example Scale

Three Categories

- Low – I'm not paying attention because I'm doing something requiring concentration (reading, conversing)
- Medium – I'm paying attention but also engaged in other activities (hiking, taking pictures)
- High – I'm actively listening (viewing, relaxing)

VOLPE center

U.S. Department of Transportation
Research and Innovative Technology Administration

Backcountry Visitor Characteristics

Attentiveness - High

- Activity – Hiking, Boating, Relaxing
- Group size – Very Small
- Presence of children in group - None
- Crowding - None

Expectations

- Previous visit experience - Varies
- Knowledge of overflights - Varies
- Reason for visit - Solitude

VOLPE center

U.S. Department of Transportation
Research and Innovative Technology Administration

Backcountry Visitor Characteristics

Are there other places where we might find visitors with these characteristics?

- *Attentiveness – Yes*
- *Expectations – Probably Not*

VOLPE center

 U.S. Department of Transportation
Research and Innovative Technology Administration

Other sites with 'Attentive' visitors?

Sites with highly attentive visitors, which are not remote and have higher visitation rates.

- Places like Audubon Centers where people listen intently for a specific sound.
- Campgrounds
- ???

VOLPE center

U.S. Department of Transportation
Research and Innovative Technology Administration

Visitor Attentiveness: Can it strengthen current relationships?

Bryce Canyon Exposure-Response Data (n=770)

1 Trail – Avg. 15-30 minutes hiking

Interference with Appreciation of Natural Quiet	Low Attentiveness (>1 Child or >3 Adults) (n=240)	Moderate Attentive (1-3 Adults) (n=530)
Did not Hear AC	84 (35%)	175 (33%)
Not at All	28 (12%)	51 (10%)
Slightly	62 (26%)	74 (14%)
Moderately	25 (10%)	95 (18%)
Very Much	26 (11%)	74 (14%)
Extremely	15 (6%)	61 (12%)

Recommendations: Alternative Exposure-Response Development Options for Backcountry Visitors

➢Develop a list of backcountry visitor characteristics.

➢ Select key characteristics which could be replicated elsewhere.

➢Analyze current data to see if relationships are strengthened when these characteristics are included as factors.

➢Find surrogate sites with similar visitor characteristics and conduct field test – large # of surveys

➢Collect a limited amount of data at backcountry sites to see if same trend is evident.

Site Selection and Noise-exposure Requirements for Studying Dose-Response

Jim Fields

Overview

- Sources of study priorities
- Basic mismatch between study design & agency needs
- Two design challenges for future studies
- Recommendations for next steps (future research)
- Assessment of questionnaire issues (if time)

Setting Study Priorities

- Depends upon
  - NPS & FAA regulatory and management needs
    - Measurement of degree of impact on visitors
    - Measurement of impact for sensitive, mission-relevant activities
    - Application to all types of areas (scenic, historical, urban)
  - State of scientific knowledge

3

Setting Priorities (Example 1): Mission-Sensitive Activities

- Possible studies
  - Activity based - noise-sensitive activities (examples)
    - Bird watching individuals or groups
    - Ranger led interpretative talks
    - Sunrise or sunset visits
  - Location based –
    - Long hikes
    - Overnight backcountry
    - Wilderness areas
    - High-altitude flights only
- Agency strategy questions affecting priority
  - Is policy only controlled by most sensitive use (i.e. overlooks are largely irrelevant for aircraft if adjacent short hike activity)?
  - Are number of visitors relevant?

4

Setting Priorities (Example 2): Historical and Cultural Sites

- Possible studies
  - Conduct dose/response site assessments at a few sites
  - Measure responses at sites with minimal noise data
- Special considerations
  - Ambient noise needs to be considered in design
  - Ambient noise conditions differ greatly (urban/rural)
  - Importance of activity varies greatly
  - Non-park road traffic can often not be ignored
- Agency strategy questions affecting priority
  - Is uniform noise metric important for administration?
  - Are acoustic resources at historical and cultural parks important or a high management priority?

5

A Fundamental Mismatch: Site visits / Park visits /Site (Management)

- Three alternative units of analysis or administration:
  - Visitors' periodic site-visits (15 minutes to several hours)
  - Visitors' park-visits (hours to days)
  - Site – the administrative unit (24 hours) – limited visitor information
- History:
  - Current site dose-response site methodology selected because only way to precisely determine noise dose
- Mismatch
  - Regulations will specify long-term site characteristics not conditions for specific visits
- Implications
  - Estimates of impact must include assumptions for at least the joint distribution of timing of visits, aircraft and ambient levels
  - The average impact at a site will be less than the impact observed under the most sensitive conditions at the site
  - Estimates of numbers of visits impacted at sites are somewhat complex as they are based on non-linear models
  - Visitors demographic characteristics may be irrelevant for routine management (group size, length of visit, expectations)
  - Total impact on a visitor's total resource experience is not know from site experiences

6

Study Design Challenge #1: Correlated Variables and Site variability

- Sites differ on a large number of variables that require multiple sites to separate effects (currently 11 sites)
  - Can not dictate variables to consider
  - Opinion survey bias : -consider individual characteristics
  - Acousticians' bias :   -consider noise characteristics
  - Managers' bias :   -consider management variables
- Random differences between sites or other groupings can dramatically increase sampling error (some current analyses ignore this and over-estimate precision)
  - Site differences
  - Time differences (day, non-acoustical site events)
  - Visitor group differences

7

Study Design Challenge #2: Design for variation within sites

- Noise index variables are most important
  - Noise exposure (of 14 sites, only 2 have more than 100 interviews outside a 10-db range in aircraft exposure)
  - Ambient noise – levels, types, difference with AC
- Dilemma – Management based on site characteristics but accuracy is best within site variation

8

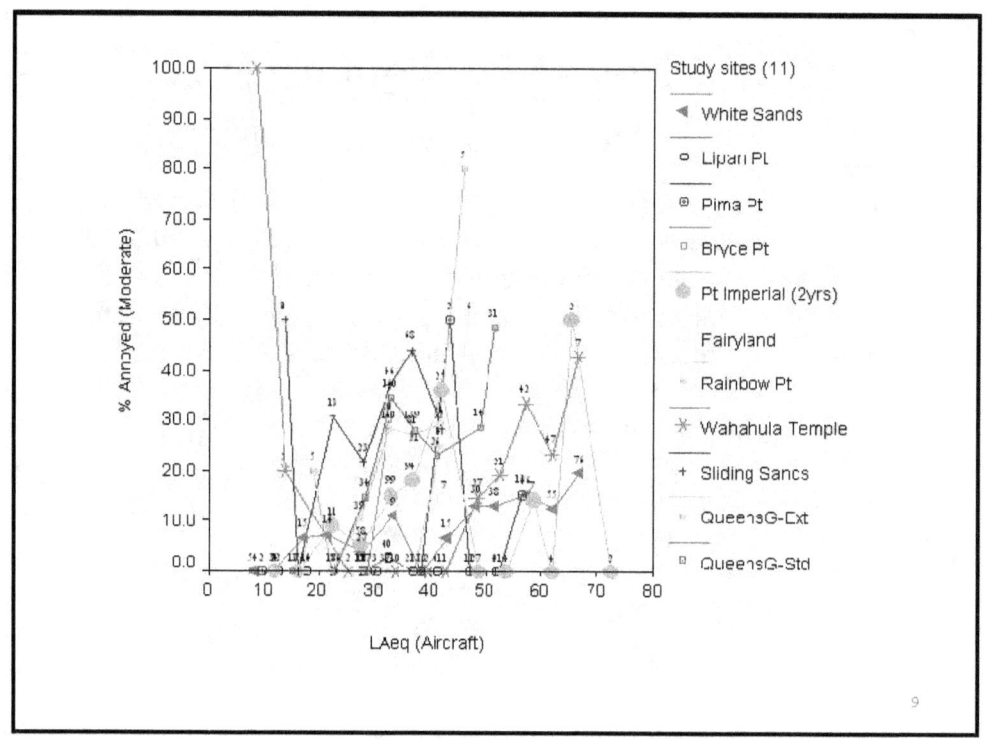

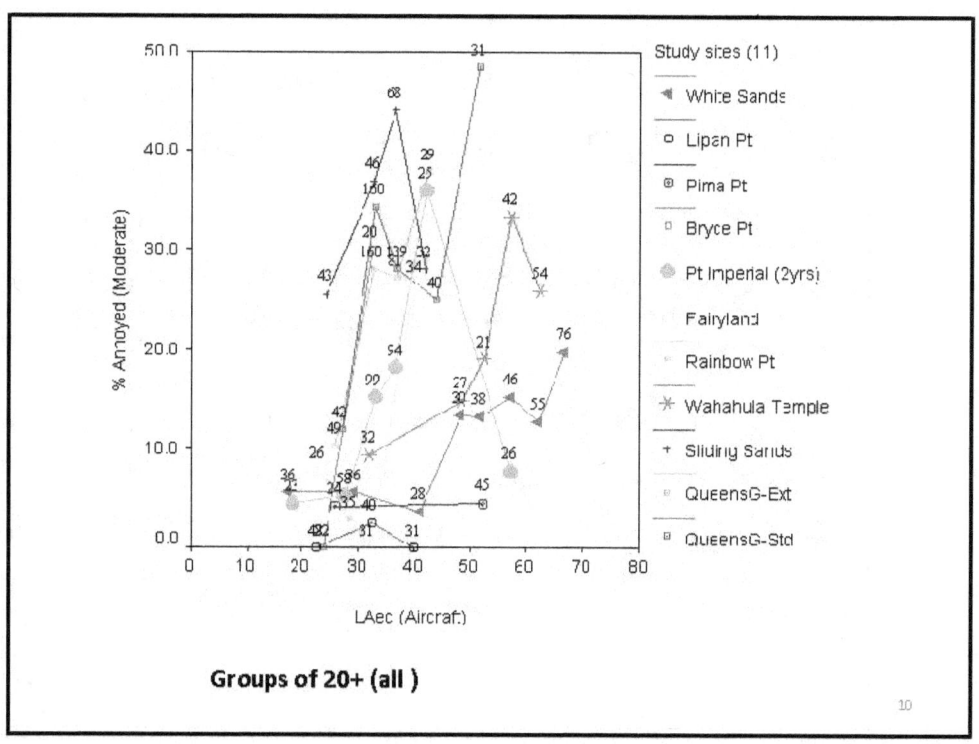

Groups of 20+ (all)

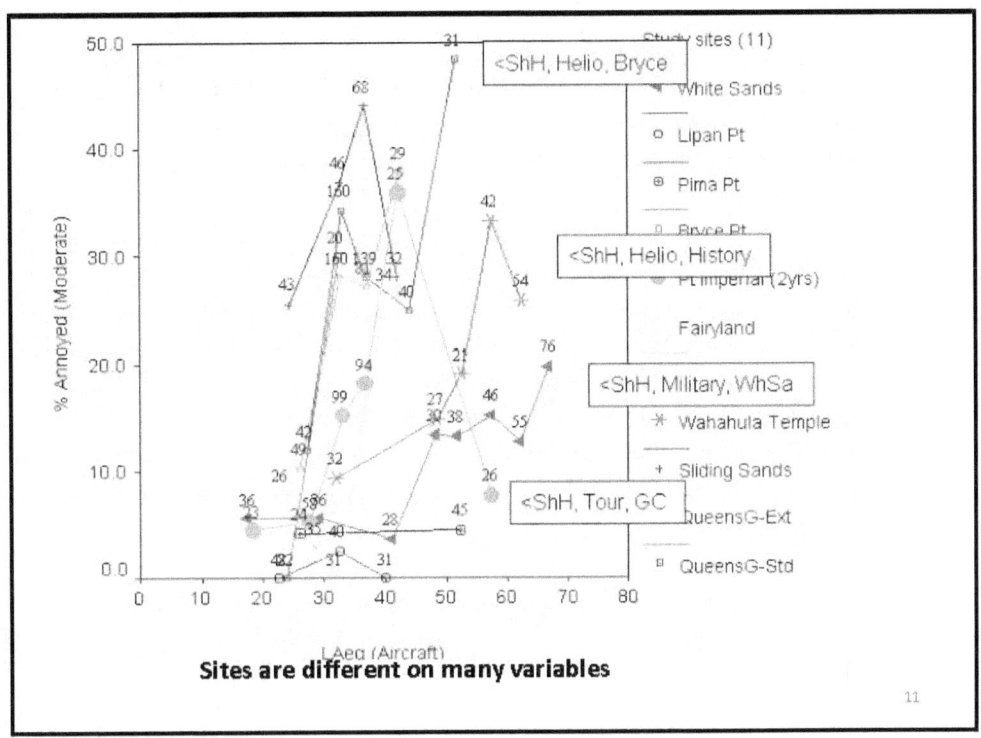

Sites are different on many variables

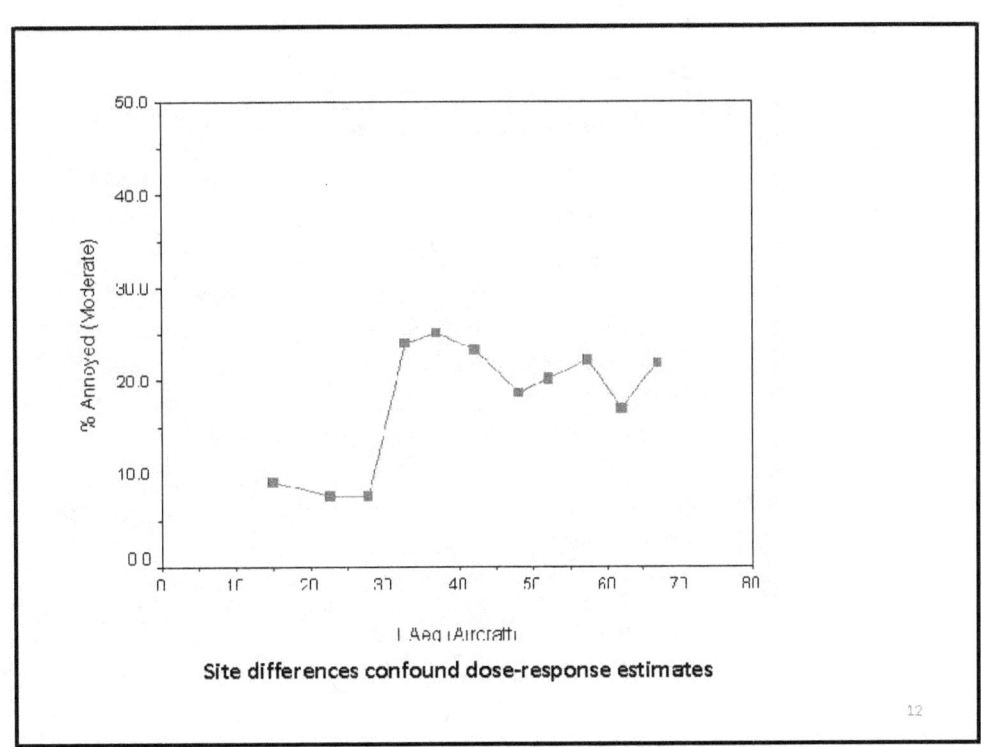

Site differences confound dose-response estimates

Current Site Characteristics
(See handout)

13

Some Lessons Learned

- Site-visit data gathering is difficult
  - Of the 14 sites where data collected
    - 3 were unusable for Volpe analysis
    - 4 more obtained fewer than 100 usable interviews
    - 5 more had a narrow exposure range (fewer than 80 interviews outside a 10-dB LAeq range)
  - Of the visitors to the sites during the study period
    - Some visitors exited without being interviewed (busy staff, etc.)
    - Of about 2,785 interviews conducted about 25% were unusable for dose/response analysis (2,112 usable)
      - 368 – missing noise data
      - 104 – Visit time did not include audible aircraft (no dose-based analysis)
      - 149 – missed answering one or more of three prime response questions

14

Recommended Next Steps

1. Assess site-visit / site management mismatch and feasibility of using current site-visit findings:
   - Test feasibility through NPS providing site characteristics data with "reasonable" effort
   - Test accuracy of site based assessment against observed summed reactions at study sites
2. Perform an analysis of all existing US data (11 sites, 2,000+ interviews) with full involvement of stakeholders (FAA, NPS) and range of consultants
   - Agree on design of analysis
   - Identify policies that are affected by specific values of outcomes
   - Estimate parameters of models and precision of estimates (i.e. regression not correlation)
   - Calculate sampling errors using appropriate cluster sampling techniques
   - Jointly review results & re-visit implications for policy
   - Derive estimates of response variation to use for future study designs (site, day, group, effects)

15

Next Steps (Continued)

3. Set precise statistical requirements for future studies with FAA & NPS working individually, together and with consultants to determine:
   - What actions and policies will be affected by study results
   - What topics are to be studied and what values of statistical estimates will result in different policy decisions
   - How precise the statistical estimates need to be
4. Develop a survey design evaluation tool to estimate the likely precision for estimates from any proposed study design
   - Measures of response variation to be derived from current NPS studies
   - World-class, survey design statistician consultant needed

16

Next Steps (Continued)

5. Gather information on potential sites that would provide the strongest design considering:
   - Characteristics of existing sites such as
     - Visitor numbers
     - Visitor activities (sensitivity etc)
     - Aircraft and ambient noise environment
     - Possibility of observing variations in policy variables within site
     - All confounding study location characteristics
   - Alternatives to current dose/response site-visit strategy:
     - Evaluate complete visits (especially backcountry)
     - Manipulate noise exposure for design or measurement cost purposes
     - Use longer-term, average estimates of site noise exposure
     - Reduce costs of noise program
   - Non NPS sites:
     - In USA
     - International cooperation in other countries

17

Next Steps (Continued)

6. Evaluate alternative designs and research projects using statistical design tool

7. Choose projects OR revise policy goals or study plans or assumptions to form new study designs

18

Basic Reaction Questions

- 7. Did you hear any airplanes, jets, helicopters, or any other aircraft during your visit to (NAME OF SITE)?
  - 1 No
  - 2 Yes

- [The next question is only for people who heard aircraft sounds here at (NAME OF SITE)."]

- 10. Were you bothered or annoyed by aircraft noise during your visit to (NAME OF SITE)? Were you
- not at all annoyed, slightly annoyed, moderately annoyed, very annoyed, or extremely annoyed by
- aircraft noise?
  - 1 Not at all annoyed
  - 2 Slightly annoyed
  - 3 Moderately annoyed
  - 4 Very annoyed
  - 5 Extremely annoyed

- 11. How much did the sound from aircraft interfere with each of the following aspects of your visit at (NAME OF SITE)? Did the sound from aircraft interfere with your (READ EACH STATEMENT) not at all, slightly, moderately, very much, or extremely?

- enjoyment of the site
- appreciation of the natural quiet and sounds of nature at the site
- appreciation of the historical and/or cultural significance of the site

19

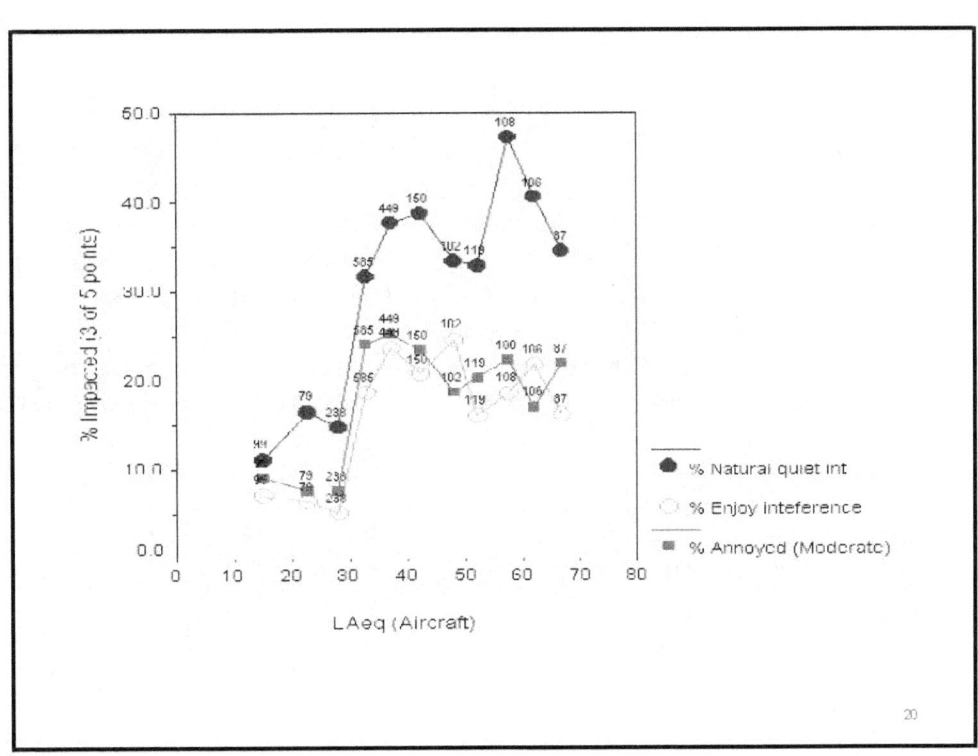

20

Conclusions about Questionnaire

- Changes to basic response questions are not recommended
  - Questions were carefully tested
  - Strict comparability is needed to maintain a data series
  - Changes in questions would be of minor importance for evaluating noise-dose indices
  - Questionnaire changes will not remove basic policy/subjective judgments
    - Will not generate reliable points of inflection
    - Variations in reactions will always give diverse answers with resulting requirement for arbitrary regulatory definitions of "impact"
- Questionnaire wording affects number of visitors counted as "affected"
- Context question for site might improve and reduce aircraft reports when no exposure
- Expectation question might be improved
- Sensitive activity classification might identify at-risk groups

21

Expectation Question

- 6. How important was each of the following reasons for your visit to (NAME OF SITE)? Would you say that (READ EACH REASON) was not at all important , slightly, moderately , very, or extremely important for your visit . (CIRCLE ONE NUMBER FOR EACH REASON)

- viewing the natural scenery was . . .
- enjoying the natural quiet and sounds of nature was ....
- appreciating the history and cultural significance of the site was...

22

Simple Enjoyment
(aircraft noise not mentioned)

- 3. Overall, how enjoyable has your visit been at (NAME OF SITE)? Has your visit been not at all, slightly, moderately, very, or extremely enjoyable? (CIRCLE ONE NUMBER)
  - 1 Not at all enjoyable
  - 2 Slightly enjoyable
  - 3 Moderately enjoyable
  - 4 Very enjoyable
  - 5 Extremely enjoyable

23

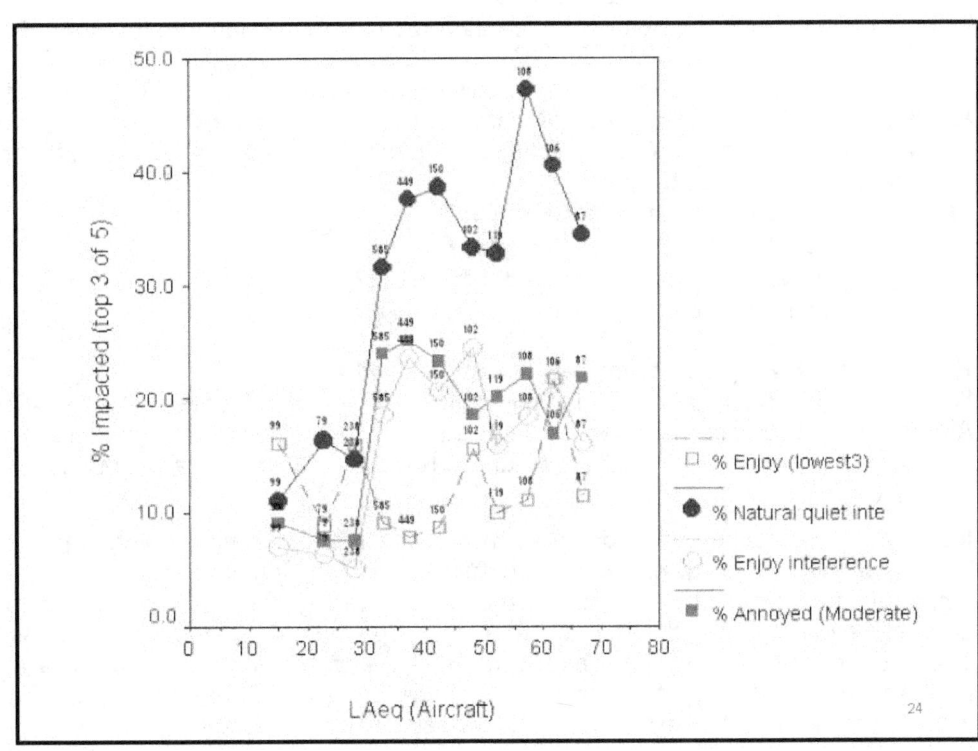

24

 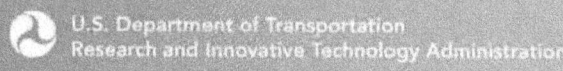

Appendix B – Meeting Notes

Day 1

Introductory Remarks

FAA: Western Pacific Region
The reason for this gathering is to create a roadmap for visitor experience and to obtain guidance from experts. Ideally a framework should guide reasonable scientific methods to analyze aircraft impacts at national parks.

- There are two NEPA actions that have lead us to look at impacts to visitor experience:
  - **Grand Canyon:** where there is a plan to restore the "natural quiet"
  - **Air Tour Management Plan (ATMP):** Congress in 2000 directed FAA and NPS to conduct an air tour program for any parks with air tour overflights
- First ATMPs at Badlands and Mount Rushmore are almost ready for review and there are also ATMPs underway in Hawaii (Hawaii Volcanoes, Haleakala)
- FAA seeks a consensus on noise metrics.
- Data gaps exist and should be filled.

FAA: Aviation Energy and Environment (AEE)
AEE is assisting with the technical oversight to assist the progress
Significance has to be analyzed by context and magnitude
FAA and NPS agree that the noise impacts to natural soundscape should be assessed within park boundaries
65 dB (maximum decibel level) is the metric FAA uses for most analysis – it is understood that this metric is inadequate for national parks.
Visitor experience has many facets/variables to consider
- Survey combined with noise data results will provide a better idea of how noise affects visitors

GOAL – to measure and model noise exposure with how the noise affects visitors in parks
Roadmap – gather a reliable body of "data" that provide guidance on next steps.
The workshop discussion should identify the weaknesses and strengths of different methodologies
Questions to be answered:
- Is there a common noise metric?
- What are the impact thresholds?
- What mitigation measures are possible?

Research alignment is critical

FAA: Airports (Prepared Comments from Jake Plante)
I'd like to thank Raquel and AEE for inviting me here on behalf of the Airports Office. Over the years, Airports has done numerous studies on noise over parks, including: Homestead, Halls Crossing, Flagstaff, St. George, Mammoth, and current projects at Mesquite and Ivanpah in Nevada, and Haley, Idaho.

It's great to see the process moving again. This workshop is important in many ways – and because these times tend to be "windows of opportunity" that don't last forever. Solving this problem requires a careful balancing act between aviation and park management. At its heart, the problem is about compatible land use. And that's why concentrating so much on noise metrics has been unproductive. The real focus should be on noise criteria – a series of dose-response curves applied to representative park land uses based on management and ambient zoning. But under any approach, we need to get back to the basics. And by basics I mean science.

Let me discuss metrics for a moment. To my colleagues in the park service, we agreed with you that DNL was not an appropriate metric for parks analysis. Now we're asking you to reconsider audibility.

This metric isn't working. Nothing wrong with the theory but the application is poor science at best. I bring this up here because we've got to ask ourselves whether audibility should be a dose-response metric for noise criteria. Yes, it came up relatively strong in the field studies because this work is observer based. But that doesn't translate into the applied science – with limited models and internal noise logic.

So there is no doubt about airports' concerns, let me cite the data. At St. George, the audibility overpredictions for cumulative operations were up to 400% above the total time in a day. And if that isn't bad enough, we're getting over 500% overprediction of audibility in our second full application. For our project-only analysis, the numbers are questionable too – just in the other direction. The audibility analysis is showing that new airport projects are making national parks quieter, *quieter surprisingly*, contrary to every other metric.

We also have no confidence in the quick fix "compression algorithm", which simply "shoehorns" bad data into a percentage and doesn't account for local operations, scheduling, and sound characteristics. So, the result of using audibility is meaningless numbers – a waste of valuable time and taxpayer dollars. Better science is needed – the audibility experiment has run its course – we need a moratorium on audibility until a formal validation is done. Maybe such work can be done here.

Let me turn to criteria development. This meeting marks a fresh start. This is a complex policy area but that doesn't mean we can't take some immediate steps. The example that comes to mind is air quality and the issue of aircraft particulates. There, FAA issued a general "first order approximation". This methodology keeps improving and it's now in its third iteration. EPA and the international community were skeptical at first and now they like it.

Where can we take some steps? Let me suggest a few priorities:

First, let's look at visitor annoyance, the key impact, and let other possible impacts wait, such as wildlife.

Second, let's look at park land use designations and how the NPS and other resource agencies can develop standardized guidance in this area. It needs to be national, not case-by-case. For example, EPA designates nonattainment areas nationally, and FAA uses 65 DNL and land use categories nationally. It can be done for park land use and noise.

Third, let's look at conventional noise metrics that are reliable and cost-effective. From the d-r studies, two metrics that jump out in some sort of combination are time above and Leq.

Is there a perfect metric? No. But we don't have a perfect metric in the airport environment. DNL does a great job for equitable land use decisions. Yet, because of its limitations, we encourage supplemental metrics to better inform the public and decision makers. Maybe this approach has some relevancy for parks.

managed the FAA parks program in the 1990's and the two FAA dose-response studies. The NPS wanted these studies initially and I want to thank the NPS again for its help in getting us into the parks and doing the work. These studies came out well – so did combining FAA studies with earlier NPS studies – but more data are needed.

Back country is a real problem - as we discovered in scoping an area of the grand canyon. But that's a good discussion to have again.

My involvement now is managing airport studies. Let me emphasize that our standard NEPA studies are not ATMPs. There are 3 distinct arenas: NEPA, ATMPs, and Grand Canyon – all with different ground rules.

Thankfully, I'm no longer on the hook for noise methodology, but we're lucky to have Raquel's skilled leadership for the FAA, and the resources to do more work. Again, thanks for inviting airports to be here, and we look forward to the new effort.

VOLPE center   The National Transportation Systems Center   U.S. Department of Transportation
Research and Innovative Technology Administration

NPS

NPS representatives provided some context regarding air tours and their impact on visitor experience at specific parks:

Grand Canyon

- Many Air tours – fixed routes and altitudes, have had a long duration of process. Involved with EIS with Grand Canyon working group and have a range of alternatives and there is an NPS preferred alternative.
- Impact analysis is in the early stages.
- Quiet technology is one of the mandates – quiet technology may allow some aircraft to be eligible for exemption if certain noise criteria are met.
- Definition of substantial restoration of natural quiet at Grand Canyon
  - 50% or more of the park achieving restoration of natural quiet – no aircraft for 75-100% of the flight day.
  - Flight day means during the day (not evening/night)
  - Restrictions are for all aircraft flying below 18,000 ft.
- Technical team formed with 8 members looking at the scientific methods to identify impact thresholds and assessing the criteria.
- NPS has already:
  - conducted expert panels on visitor experience and wildlife
  - Submitted a preferred alternative for the rule making process.
- NPS is required to mitigate impacts wherever possible and supposed to categorize impacts into a range of impacts (negligible, minor, moderate, significant).
- Denali
  - Park is exempt from the ATMP
  - From a Denali visitor perspective, the number 1 complaint was weather prior to 10 years ago. Now the number 1 complaint among visitors is aircraft.
- Grand Teton
  - Dealing with the challenges related to the large commercial airport within the boundaries of the park.

Background on Current FAA/NPS Dose-Response Data Part I
Nick Miller

- Began dose-response work in 1991 – the approach has been adopted by other groups
- Became familiar with dose response work from work with residential communities
- Park is a "different" sound environment – normal assessment methods might not be applicable
- Field team had to use special noise equipment as most equipment won't capture below 20 dB.
- Work at Haleakala - previous work involved a researcher who recorded how often he could hear aircraft within a park.
- At the time could gather 1-second A-weighted levels.
- Survey team used annoyance as it is used for most transportation communities. Annoyance levels were moderately, very, and extremely annoyed
- Short questionnaire as the visitors visit parks for a brief amount of time.

Mediators

- Had difficulty with determining type of aircraft, as our equipment couldn't distinguish so assumed that visitors would also not be able to distinguish.
- All visitor activity was outdoors to ensure that they did not hear indoor noise that could influence responses.
- Used Point Imperial at the Grand Canyon – could observe visitors at the location, the duration of the visit, and then interview the visitor.

Short hikes – definition: people would have to walk 5-10 minutes

 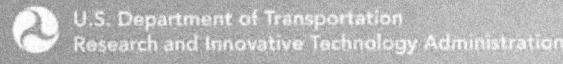

- We realized that background noise is an important feature because it affects audibility, and how much aircraft stands out from other noise.

Interference with "natural quiet" if this is a management objective
- Rather than interference with "enjoyment" with this technique, you have to ask a specific example to elicit information about a specific area.
- People report that scenery is the first concern and soundscape is second according to transcripts from congressional hearings

Conducted other analysis at White Sands
Researchers asked the following question – "What if we told people to expect impacts"
Created signs that read: "Military aircraft can be regularly seen and heard on this walk"
- Only 40% saw and remembered the sign – if you want them to do something you can't expect them to read or think! You have to help them.
- If you can't control the noise you can inform the visitors and adjust their expectations
- Sensitivity varies from site to site, (see slides)
- At white sands researchers gathered more information about interference vs. annoyance and different levels.
- Researchers learned that aircraft traveling together reduces annoyance.

Researchers need policy experts to determine where is your threshold of impact – it is a policy issue to decide threshold as the data will not necessarily give you the answer – science will only reveal relationships.

Questions/Answers:

1. Question: Have researchers considered a "Noise free interval" metric? – in one pervious study visitors to Shenandoah episodes of not seeing people they experience was deemed a wilderness interval.
Answer: Some of the metrics currently utilized may provide a substitute for a "noise-free interval"
2. Question: Has Interference with Natural Quiet vs. Enjoyment been considered:
Answer: Amanda (Rapoza) found there wasn't a large difference between annoyance and enjoyment

Background on Current FAA/NPS Dose-Response Data Part II
Amanda Rapoza

Volpe went to Bryce in 1997 to collect short hike data
Bryce seemed like an ideal site due to its large number of visitors and proximity to aircraft.
- Looking for a "holy grail" of acoustic descriptors
- 905 data points with good surveys and good noise data
- Change in exposure was a new acoustic descriptor
- Received sound level of data across the entire range time above"0-100%"
- Typically, 20% of respondents will report annoyance even with no (zero) acoustic dose.
- Factors include: context, time in environment, response metrics in that time of environment
- Team was looking for simplicity – hoping that national management plans could be developed with dose-response findings
- Tried to avoid presence of children, large groups, and "repeat" visitors.

1998 visited overlooks in an effort to explore different sorts of descriptors for different settings/contexts
- Went back to Point Imperial, and back to Bryce for overlooks. Short hike visitors were the most annoyed user group
- We looked at the data points looked at tour aircraft
- Wanted to develop combined relationships
- Percent Time Above Ambient (%TAA) was best descriptor

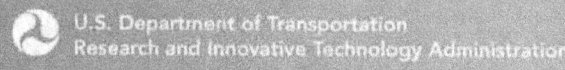

- Looked at different response high altitude aircraft vs. tour aircraft. Tour Aircraft had higher annoyance.
- Mediator of first visit or repeat visit, looked at the duration visitors were in the park in the first place
- Overlooks and short hikes yield statistically significant differing results.

Questions/Answers:

1. Question: With longitudinal surveys (1992 and 1999) were there differences in exposures?
Answer- Don't recall
2. Question: Were there differences in R-squares (differences in the variation)?
Answer: -Can't recall at this moment

What additional information can be mined from the current data?
Grant Anderson

We are not asking that data explains every person's annoyance only looking for the correct percentage (only looking for a percentage with visitors) same number of over counts and undercounts

- Combined database 2 years at Grand Canyon, Hawaii Parks, Bryce, White Sands, and other locations.
- Splitting point (dichotomous relationships) between moderate and very annoyed etc.
- Some of the mediators have to deal with individual and the site
- Raw data done separately by aircraft type
- Eliminate the "shoulders" of the visit – first 5 minutes are not necessarily important to their visit.
- There is precision potentially possible with dose-response
- Noise free intervals can be augmented
- % Time above ambient
- Site differences (non of this is in database) e.g. Trail length, average duration
- Explore data
- Use plots and many graphics (correlation coefficients) **See slides**
- Improve/Expand upon the analysis
  - % time audible, relative LAeq add both into the analysis at the same time.
  - Many have to know 2 factors and create a compound dose. What was the LAeq when the aircraft was audible?
  - Low S/N stands for Signal Noise
  - Can keep two metrics separate using LAeq and %TAA
  - Multi-level – runs the risk of producing correlation when interviewing multiple people in the same party.

Session 1

What do Park Managers Need to Effectively Manage Air Tours
Frank Turina

Speaker wanted to place current workshop in the broader context of NPS decision making
- General Authority (Organic Act; Redwoods Act)
  - Sole authority for managing the resources – dichotomy with enjoying the resource, while also protecting simultaneously
  - What is significant vs. non-significance
- MPs Management Plans (MP) are guidance documents (MP 4.9 - Soundscape)
- National Parks Overflights Act – Grand Canyon

 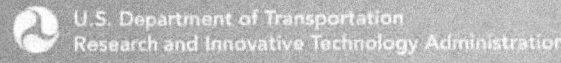

- Many times we don't have a good understanding of the variables and there is also high uncertainty associated (certain times it can be challenging)
- Makes it difficult to determine impacts due to the variation between parks. Some notable variables:
  - Appropriate vs. inappropriate use of park
  - Types of visitors and visitor experience
  - Management objectives we have management zones for each park
- Visitor Experience and Resource Protection (VERP) visitor experience resource protection we do consider park visitors on snow mobiles and aircraft visitors
- Role for Professional Judgment – how we set standards and make decisions
  - Decision or opinion that is shaped by education/training/experience
  - Advice or insights
  - Good science/scholarship
  - Public involvement
- NPS is decentralized
  - Many decisions made at park level
  - Additional decisions made at the regional level

Science has key role informing National Park Service
- Objective & Transparent
- Incorporates professional judgment, expertise
- MP 4.1 – In cases of uncertainty, the protection of natural resources must predominate. If we don't understand impacts we will err on side of protecting resources.
- MP 8.11.2 – NPS will use best available science
- MP 2.3.1.4 – Decisions have to made by good science
- National Parks Omnibus Management Act of 1998 – professional judgment is part of the consideration
- DO12/NEPA – based on good scientific data
- We rely on science to influence our policy decisions.

Questions/Answers:

1. Question: when superintend leaves what happens with the decision making?
Answer: many issues remain constant; may be slight differences in management philosophies but changes should be minimal. Decision making is based on previous direction so it is difficult to change.

2. Question: is there a possibility that even with a determination of a "threshold" it will change with superintends?
Answer: not likely – superintendents have been very "park" focused and really look at the specifics of their parks.

Human Dimensions of Park Soundscapes: Recent Research and Recommendations for Future Directions – Part I, II, III
Part I – Robert Manning

Park and outdoor management frameworks – managing noise and soundscapes
This presentation doesn't directly reference aircraft noise – uses other noises analogous to aircraft noise

Management Frameworks:
- Limits of Acceptable Change (LAC)
- VERP (is almost the exact same guidance as LAC)
- Formulate management objectives/desired condition
- Standards of quality are maintained they must monitor indicators

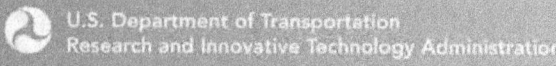
- Apply management practices as they pertain

Muir Woods National Monument
- Determine indicators of quality (quantitative & qualitative) - Sound was mentioned as a priority
  - Noisy visitors annoyed them the most (4th most important annoyance in ranking)
- What is it that determine what noise
- Normative methods – wanted to establish standards (what are the qualities that visitors desire) have been able to help establish thresholds.
- Noise at 37 dB - the point at which the soundscape is at marginal quality.
- Visitor surveys - are methods to monitor the sound related qualities of visitors –
  - Could limit # or sensitive other visitors
  - Created "quiet zone" in Cathedral Zone
  - Created "quiet days" vs. control periods
  - Visitors were generally highly supportive of management actions.
- Most of work has been completed one park at a time and need a systemic approach
- Normative model of human-caused noise (developed a diagram of relationships between crowding and noise) **see slides**
- Many factors including some visitors who may not visit the parks due to soundscape degradation
- Natural sounds contributed to the experience

Questions/Answers:

1. Question: does crowding ever increase acceptability?
Answer: sometimes slightly higher levels of "crowding" as more acceptable.
2. Question: why use acceptability?
Answer: Might choose another term now, but sometimes surveys use "preference" or .how bad would it have to get to deter visitation/displacement" Another proxy question is: "what should NPS manage for?"
3. Question: How do you fit in the concept that the visitors' expectations might not be aligned with the purpose of the site?
Answer: NPS can work to set up reasonable expectations – there can be a disconnect between the NPS viewpoints and the visitors.

Part II
Steve Lawson

Personal Background – 10 years of NPS related research, more recently connected with soundscape back in 2006 with NPS workshop. Systems modeling and noise modeling in National Parks.

Haleakala / Hawaii Volcanoes
- Summer 2007 – Data Collection at Haleakala and Hawaii Volcanoes
- Involved two types of surveys – audio recordings & attended listening
- Attended listening – intercepted park visitors at the study sites
- Participants sat for 3-5 minutes and listened (modern society is virtually unable to sit and listen for more than 30 seconds). Gave them a check list to check and rate the acceptability in that area of the park. Asked for open ended descriptions of any feeling that was associated with the experience. Surveyors recorded the presence of aircraft at the time.
- Haleakala on average graded noise just below neutral 0.4 on a 4 point +/- scale
- Listened to five recordings and used an acceptability scale. (played 5 levels of sound)
- Had noise cancelling headphones and played audio clips prepared by Kurt Fristrup
- Hearing helicopters more than once during every hour has a negative impact on experience
- Visitors notice helicopters – visitors consider exposure more than once an hour unacceptable.
- Haleakala natural quiet was the highest factor cited for visitation and aircraft noise the highest detractor from the experience
- Evaluation of context – work on overlooks vs. short hikes

- The following additional work would be interesting:
  1. Measurement of frequency of "hearing a sound"
  2. In Grand Canyon putting noise levels in the context of other noise sources/environments
  3. Integration of visitor use considerations for different parks/areas
  4. Non-market valuation of soundscapes
  5. GPS and portable recording devices
  6. Visual-based assessment of high altitude flights

Part III
Britton Mace (Called in from external site due to flight cancellation)

- Background – in 1993 started to pursue helicopters visual and auditory impacts
- Asked the following question: "How to we evaluate different types of landscapes" – I wanted to apply the methodology to landscape evaluation and aesthetics
- Recorded sound and brought it back to a research facility to control environment.
- Used noise and slides in a room to assess responses. Sound was presented for 30 seconds along with a visual depiction (**See PowerPoint slides** for detailed methodology)
- Nature scenes and sounds are rated higher in preferences than other areas – deserts are rated lower
- Findings suggest that there are different results for each park.
- Source Attribution – noise – just the presence of the helicopter is a cause of annoyance
- **See PowerPoint presentation** for other related studies – helicopters were noticed most often
- Plan is to begin an audibility study
- Future research dose/response could be expanded
- It would be useful to compare jets vs. helicopters
- Vary the audible, LAeq, Lmax, # of encounters
- Lab research could also be conducted for different management zones
  o Subjects in the role of visitor to GCNP back country
- Identify acoustic zones in parks and collect sound recordings and attended logging data from these zones, followed by combination with visitor surveys
  o Visitor surveys
  o Pre/Post at St. George Airport
- Observational methods visitor tracking at viewpoints in parks affected by aircraft overflights.

Questions/Answers:

1. Question: Audio participants listen for how long and have they been compared to field research?
Answer: 30-45 seconds of sound and the results are correlated between lab data and onsite – the variable rating scales are important for the visitors. This same lab work has been used in the residential development arena for many years.

How can the value of the wilderness experience be defined and measured?
Bill Borrie

US Department of Agriculture (USDA) and US Fish and Wildlife Service (FWS) funded
- Single item (ie. Noise) measures don't fare very well with surveys
- Looking at alternative measures for methodologies
- Post-hoc vs. in-situ
  o Visitors and respondents don't have complete cognitive access to thoughts and feelings if they are measured off site – reliable recall may be beyond cognitive ability.
  o Responses become attuned to cultural norms.
  o Selective attention to what we attend to.

- o We tend to blur over specific events and we use "generic" evaluations
- o Often people will provide the most plausible answer.
- o Will use a past experience – mood becomes a proxy.
- o Ordering the questions will have an impact
- o The most taxing the questions the more participants will tailor their response
- o Visitors have provided high satisfaction ratings in surveys
- o We are managing for outstanding experiences instead of measuring for annoyance – too difficult to process all the events, etc.
- o Group dynamics (group size, presence of children, other visitors, environmental context) affect results
- o Limits of acceptable change – identify the qualities to be preserved and the indicators of quality. Set the standards of acceptability
- • Worthwhile to discuss what is a good indicator:
  - o What are the most significant indicators of the experience or on-site conditions?
  - o Visitor experiences are not necessarily goal directed or prescribed.
  - o Place for qualitative research to document which qualities are most influential (can't separate the Soundscape from the rest of the experience)
  - o What qualities?
    - ▪ Yellowstone (x-country skiers/snow mobiles/snow coaches). Groups are more similar than they are different when describing their goals (wildlife, natural scenery, learning, etc.)
    - ▪ Risk and uncertainty of outcomes Gates of the Arctic
    - ▪ **See PowerPoint** for other studies
- • Definition of Wilderness is necessary guide on characteristics for experience

Research needs:
- • In-situ, multi-method
- • Validation across different parks

Questions/Answers:

1. Question: can you give an example of qualities as opposed to single indicators?
Answer: the trip was challenging, unique setting, experiences can be not be experienced anywhere else.
Set of questions many of the observations you observe may be influenced by the types of studies.
2. Question: How strongly do feel about the immediacy of a response?
Answer: if you can get closer to the experience you can better document it.

General Discussion and summary of key ideas from Session 1

Still can work with the data – especially using the raw data.
- • Mine existing data (squeeze) to assess if there is a pattern, can we account for context
- • The way we would gather data in the future – 1/3 or 1/8 octave dB is sufficient
- • Any technique has to be able to control for noise exposure (we have to know that the noise isn't correlating with other variables).
- • Nick – is there a way we could have a white paper to combine sociology with the acoustic dose response. How does a recreational sociologist characterize a certain site?
- • Have to have an integrated – study plans or problem analysis. Joint papers authored by a recreational sociologists and acousticians.
- • We have a set of sites with sophisticated acoustical data, but not much data on how the sites can be characterized.
- • Much work has been done on the independent variable "side of things" and sociologists have done work on the dependent variable "side of things".

 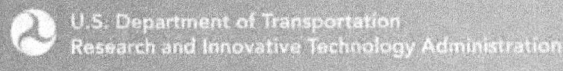

- A list of 10 measures where aircraft create impact – could inform decision makers. If we set the threshold at a discrete level we could examine the effects. Questions include: what are the effects on Visitor; what are the cumulative impacts?

Comments:

NPS – The more studies we can consider the more valid our final decision (the more information we get the better).

FAA – It is ideal if these impacts can be quantified in some way either via models or other measures. Propose to keep the data collection goals practical so that findings can be applied to the ATMP program.

Session 2

Data Gaps in Dose-Response Work
Nick Miller

- We only have done aircraft and maybe we can learn a lot from conducting other types of noise measurements
- There is resistance to set a threshold because we don't know what the impacts will be on visitors or air tours.
- The value of decision makers conducting acoustic site visits:
  - It is very informative to do an hour of logged listening with decision makers – Possibility to create an experience at a number of sites and with the decision makers taking notes and the acousticians measuring everything.
  - Only after you have conducted these studies will the metric make sense for the policy makers.
  - Only with the assistance of the acoustician can there by adequate identification of Soundscape resource.
  - For example with air pollution – you can provide people with an assessment with parts per million data (pollutant concentrations in air), but unless you show them a photo (with the airborne pollution visible) they won't understand.

Comments:

NPS – you can't solely use the current assessment because a visitor may see the air quality as excellent, but it actually may be marginal from a planning perspective or historical conditions.

FAA – We manage to protect the resource, but we don't manage specially for visitor preference.
  - Whatever process that is adopted should be consistent from park to park.
  - Protecting the park is important, should try to make it systematic so that FAA can meet NPS goals.

Dose-Response Site selection based on Natural Soundscape Resource Protection.
Dick Horonjeff

Organic Act specifies protecting specific resource within a park as an independent resource.

- Do we look at this a separate recreational vs. soundscape opportunity
- The basic premise: Separate dose response curves
- Primary consideration: Is visitor reaction related to a generalized non-auditory based recreational opportunity?

 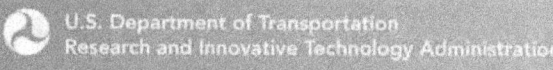
- Is the particular soundscape related to a overall recreational opportunity (extreme quiet, animal sounds, waterfall, etc.)
- Multiple soundscapes may exist within a single recreational opportunity.
- Uncertainty associated with impacts may be from the types of opportunity each visitor receives. Or, it could be from the fact that multiple soundscapes may be available for some observers and not others.
- If multiple soundscapes exist should they each be managed differently?
- Determine what they are and design to the most sensitive worth preserving.
- Soundscapes can be transient in nature – while soundscapes are available can these resources by protected?
  1. Determine locations where these opportunities exist. (specific conditions, when they occur, etc.)
  2. Identify when these soundscapes could be impaired
  3. Manage the soundscape enjoyment
- Specific soundscape opportunity – could be anything from extreme quiet all the way up to the rapids in the Colorado River.
- Visitors will have unique response to impairment
- Curves – instead create dose-response curves for different soundscapes not use types (e.g. overlooks/short hikes).

Questions/Answers:

1. Question: Do visitors have the sophistication to make these soundscape distinctions?
Answer: Uncertain
2. Question: Should we study different sensitivities to different soundscapes?
Answer: NPS is managing for opportunities for visitors to experience a certain sound environment.

Major data gaps: How can they be resolved?
Grant Anderson

Backcountry activities – Exploration of how the backcountry visitor experience can be evaluated.
- Challenges:
  o Each visitor: different doses/responses over an extended visit (several weeks)
  o Hiker location/activity: hour by hour
- Need for thorough hiker responses: sufficiently thorough
- Harder to measure the doses – suggestion to do it sufficiently

Different doses hour by hour
- Does it depend on the activity?
- Does it depend on the particular soundscape?
- Can we control for the hiker?
- Attach track sticks to backpack
  o Small light weather-proof, requires easily obtainable AAA batteries
  o Month of hourly locations stored internally
  o Hiker "log" each night
  o Activity by hour, when did they notice aircraft
  o Want to know if there will be some habituation
- Won't be able to hide that this will be a noise study
- Interview at the end of hike:
  o Compute the dose rather than measuring it
  o Provide them with monetary ($500?) incentive
  o Conduct hiking close to FAA radar towers.

Run real contours, requires nearby radar and relatively level terrain.

 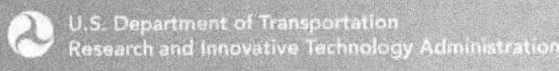

- Compute hourly contours, each day
- May require "spotters" to identify air tours
- Can compute Aircraft LAeq and % Time Audible
- Give each backpacker a weather proof sound-meter and we post process to get the self noise out. Can store 0.1 second LAeq.
- Could we measure the noise dose well enough hour by hour and then we can watch the person walk through them?

Comment:

Volpe Center - this approach would not get air tour data from FAA radar stations relevant to most parks

Alternative Exposure-Response Measurement Options
Amanda Rapoza

- Don't have enough data for backcountry areas – is there another place we can simulate the backcountry visitor somewhere else?
- 2 Groupings:
  - Attentiveness (Activity, Group size, presence of children in group, crowding)
  - Expectations
- Three categories: Low, Medium, High levels of attentiveness
- Are there other places where we can find visitors with these characteristics?
  - Attentiveness – yes; Expectations – no
  - Sites with highly attentive visitors, which are not remote and have higher visitation rates
- Bryce Canyon Groupings (low attentiveness) vs. (medium attentiveness) based on group size

Question and Answer:

Question – What is so difficult about conducting back country studies?
Answer - It is all about the obtaining and measuring the "dose."

Site Selection and noise-exposure requirements for studying dose-response
Jim Fields

Site Selection and Noise
- NPS & FAA regulatory needs
- Possible studies
- Activity Studies vs. Location Based
- Management – Mismatch between model to predict how impacted people are for a time duration
  - Park visit as a whole (should some activities be weighted?)
  - 14 to 16 studies exist and I haven't seen where they figure in policy
  - The starting point of the study is what can used to set regulations
  - If we used directly what we used from the site visit studies – we need to know the time, noise, ambient levels,
- What should we do next?
  - Sites vary and they vary in an enormous ways – what makes them different they are two helicopter sites and one is aircraft.
  - Have more variables than we can handle – different time of day. Bound to be random differences between sites – we are almost certainly overestimating the precision in our analysis.
- Not yet ready to suggest another study:
  - Look at what we have now and decide how we can use it
  - Take 14 sites characterize them and have managers determine if they can use that data?
  - Suggestion on how we can do the analysis and what should happen next.

- Set precise statistical measurements
- Develop a tool for designing next survey/study
- Find what sites are available and find out how precise the results can be from the designs.
  - Need to find ways that we can reduce cost
  - Perhaps a future study will involve running aircraft over parks
  - The eventual policy may involve a decision that doesn't involve studies.

Questions, Answers, and Comment:

1. Question: What is the best way to measure these impacts for a policy tool?
Answer: Control of the dose to establish the slopes of the dose. It is probably inadvisable to manipulate flights

General Discussion and summary of key ideas from Session 2

NPS and FAA
1) Have to provide descriptions from a management perspective identifying various management levels of "quietness."
2) How would you describe the visitor experience as it relates to the resource (e.g., "annoyance" has no meaning for NPS vs. interference with natural quiet or noise-free interval). What are the dimensions of the experience the NPS is trying to preserve?
3) What data are needed for ATMPs? What are the dimensions of the regulations? (Altitude, location, Frequency, Temporal requirements, Type of aircraft)
4) Sociologists and Acousticians have a lot of work to do. If we are going to do these studies, how do we determine site selection? Acousticians need to look at other metrics to see how they interfere with the appreciation of natural quiet.
   a. Indicators and standards – define management objectives and translate into measureable indicators.
   b. Management component – what are the approaches to managing the aircraft overflights?
   c. Create a problem analysis – what do we know about and what do we need to know?
   d. Employ multiple research methods – every research method has strengths and weaknesses. Original dose-response work – in-situ measurements led to difficulties with analyses.
   e. Take a systematic approach to study – instead of individual segmented studies, take a program approach. Outcome would be more than the sum of its parts.
   f. Most of the discussion has been about aircraft noise - probably should go beyond and include all anthropogenic sources.

The end of this session was slightly modified - participants were divided into three groups to summarize future research needs.

Group A

3 Recommendations:
1. Prepare a white paper to help guide a new framework.
2. Identify other factors (e.g., social science considerations) for the existing sites to incorporate into analysis.
3. Examine/Identify opportunities to "piggyback" (combine) research efforts.

If the FAA and NPS have separate viewpoints on some decisions, decision-makers should elevate the issue to a higher level and combine it with supplemental analysis on a park-by-park basis.

 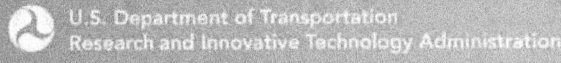
NPS – one of the real problems is that both agencies have to sign a Record of Decision (ROD) or Finding of No Significant Impact (FONSI), which makes the NEPA process more cumbersome.

Group B

How can we get better dose-response relationships?
1. White paper jointly written between an acoustician and a recreational ecologist (sociologist). Requires extensive collaboration.
    a. Team could conduct a multivariate approach with other questions so it could be jointly designed.
2. We would learn from that action – could get started the same time we would design a program to get more data and then the acoustician.
3. Thresholds should come from management and not from science. We need a system of thresholds.
4. National vs. park standard (national guidelines vs. national standards) - it is unlikely to have standards that will apply to every park and every soundscape.

Group C

Question of what kind of Visitor Experience metrics are appropriate?
- Coordinated research would provide benefits over piecemeal studies
- White Paper – could evaluate all studies and systemize and generalize across parks for management zones guided by indicators
- NPS does not "care" about number or percent "annoyed"
- NPS Park Managers can identify what experience they are trying to achieve/promote
    o Instead Researchers could focus on:
        ▪ Selection of soundscape indicators
        ▪ Flight free zones
        ▪ Seasonal-temporal zoning
        ▪ Noise free intervals
    o Interference with Natural Quiet is key impact
- Dose-response research doesn't necessarily inform NPS decisions
- Noise studies are in their infancy relative to research on solitude
- Studies findings have led to the consensus view that more than 3-5 interactions in a day interferes with the solitude experience – *is there an analogue threshold for natural quiet?*
- Additional Questions:
    o How can managers identify another threshold other than "annoyance?"
    o Solitude studies may be a useful analogue for impacts to visitors experience
    o Is there a possibility to generalize across parks?
    o How can the quantitative and qualitative research inform each others' studies?
    o Can researchers return to studies and relate noise free intervals to time periods?
    o What variables influence variations in responses?

All three groups' individual discussion (from the joint summary meeting) is provided below:

Report Out From Break Out Groups

- Reanalysis proceeds in a framework with regular research-agency consultation
- Identify other factors for the existing sites to meld into analysis
- Identify "piggy-back" (combined effort) opportunities with existing/planned research
- NPS to define (1) management objectives for resources and (2) visitor experience [and describe if these are the same or different]
- FAA to identify what decisions should be made by FAA, e.g., what decisions FAA needs to make for ATMP and what they need to do to accomplish that

The National Transportation Systems Center   U.S. Department of Transportation
Research and Innovative Technology Administration

- Sociologists to describe relationships from their research for others to be able to interpret.
- Acousticians to look at other metrics outside their research
- Develop joint white paper
- Mine existing data (from different sources)
  - Use methods from both disciplines (analysis plan)
  - Learn from methods
- Design more methodology?
  - Test/guidance in lab
  - Opportunity or experience zone
  - Test plan (follow-on)
- Identify thresholds for defined zones (Jake's methods)
  - "Acceptability" levels
- Characteristics to consider in new work/approaches
  - Indicators & Standards
    - Define, monitor, and manage
    - Determine how research will address these
  - Address needs or gaps through problem analysis and conceptual model
  - Employ multiple research methods
  - Be systematic in approach
  - Measure multiple sources of noise

Discussion summary following break-out groups:

NPS – we need to identify the data gaps even with re-analyzing existing studies
- We can quickly determine what we can get out of the existing data set – and what we couldn't find. There were a number of population data that could be mined to get better predictors.
- What can we get out an existing dataset?
- What is necessary to proceed?
  - Should keep time requirements in mind, e.g., OMB information collection requirements surrounding surveys.
  - We can spend more time looking at issues that have come up in existing ATMPs to identify potential disagreements.

Day 2

What Information can we get from the data?
Grant Anderson and Amanda Rapoza presented a summary of the content and format of the current dose-response database.

- Some of the later (dose-response) studies excluded some of the variables - they were excluded after being determined not statistically significant.
  - Data came from the survey and from observations. Various people in the group were encouraged to fill out the survey simultaneously. The interviewers were professional physiologists.
- The acoustic recordings are in 1 second intervals, but all data is A-weighted but not 1/3 octave. We have 10 year old DAT tapes and logged observations. The data were analyzed after observer log were reduced and the acoustic data was reduced.
- Should probably consider the acoustic tapes as not applicable due to their age and related concerns.
- It is recommended to look at the actual studies to better understand the survey as the listing of the questions is not sufficient to understand. Recommend a review of the questions in a smaller group as there are many details that deserve an extended discussion.

- Perhaps the "acceptability" question from the survey represents a way that the new recreational sociology research could be linked with the dose-response work.
- There are 150-200 sites with data and researchers should look at the metrics and see how closely they are correlated. We have observer logs with percent time audible.
- The Sierra Club is pushing audibility as a metric.
- Perhaps there is another metric we could use for audibility without actually using it. INM does a good job with detecting audibility.
- NPS uses a host of metrics, not just audibility.
- NPS provided strict instructions as to what constitutes a "dose" so that the research could be replicated. Researchers were in the learning process as they went through the parks and culled variables along the way.
- Researchers did not record site characteristics and with only 14 sites we don't have a degree of freedom.
- This dose-response work was completed with the acousticians and ideally next steps can incorporate the more recent data from Steve (Lawson), Bob (Manning), Britt (Mace) and Bill (Borrie).

Workshop participants were broken into two groups: Government and Technical experts. Participants in each of the "break-out" groups reported back to the entire group.

Technical Experts Break-out Group Summaries

- How do we improve the "generalizability" to broad set of places (regions, management zones, parks, etc.)
- Need guidance from NPS on management zone goals (need to know the extremes) Without these the collected data won't be comprehensive or randomly selected.
    o Need a matrix. Management objectives/site objectives/visitor types.
    o Second question is to expand the list of motivation and values (appreciation of cultural sites, scenery, and sounds) can be expanded to include family bonding, healthy experience.
    o Third question – what acoustical issues from the data set – will find that the design wasn't strong enough (e.g., sufficient number of people in a range of acoustical exposures). Key driver is the cost of doing site visits – future discussion on how to resolve costs. What is the salience of acoustic metrics (indicators) for visitor response?

- What are the strengths and weaknesses of multiple methods?
    o Dose response, audio clip, in-situ, lab, qualitative, observation, modeling
- What are the management and monitoring issues? Planning framework and management framework suggests that researchers have to monitor and take measures to ensure the methods truly ensure that parks are quieter.
- What about a physiological response – heart rate changes etc. There is work in Europe on health exposure.

Technical experts have reached the conclusion that they need to discuss this information for a couple of days.

- Re-analysis of the existing data - how to reanalyze the data.

NPS and FAA asked what would be the best way to further the future research:
Answer: (5 days of work time for each person) 2 day meeting, 2 day prep, 1 day travel. Timeline – to be accomplished ASAP.
- FAA inquired if the technical experts can assist the decision-makers with concrete numbers so that they can make determinations of adverse impacts on visitor experience.
    o Can work with Volpe to identify the barriers.

- o   Help to define what the curbs will look like.
- NPS - agency homework is somewhat dependent on what the researchers can tell us about the variations in the NPS. This isn't necessary for every type of visitor that visits a National Park. Some considerations for measurement:
    - o   Land-use – willing to consider certain parcels as homogenous for other parks
    - o   Types of Visitors.
    - o   Acoustic/listening opportunities
- NPS/FAA determined that a separate meeting (without private contractors) would be necessary to discuss funding mechanisms for future work.

2nd Breakout Session

The Technical Team – Was tasked with the 2-3 big questions that can't be addressed within the limits of this workshop.

Task 1 – Future in-person workshop
1. Define research priorities (pre-meeting prep) can pick out a few shared papers with summaries so that readers will know what to focus on?
2. 3-Day Meeting
    - Matrix with Agencies
    - Reanalysis design (High Level, Dose Response)
    - Priorities beyond reanalysis
3. Post Meeting Production
    - White paper
    - Roadmap

Task 2 – Reanalysis of Existing Data
1. Part A
    - Dose response
    - Hawaii audio clips & listening
    - Muir Woods program of research
    - Yellowstone
    - Yosemite & Grand Teton listening
    - Lab studies (Mace and Bell)

2. Draft and final report
3. Meeting to present & discuss findings and next steps (would like NPS input throughout the process)

NPS will coordinate with Nick so that "we" can do some sweeping across the data (by the time of the George Wright Conference).

Participants agreed that workshop proceedings posted on the KSN network would be sufficient and CD-ROMs are not necessary.

Government break-out summary (note: discussion of procurement strategies is not included in this set of proceedings)

General Observations:
- Too late into process to incorporate any new Dose-Response findings into Mount Rushmore Environmental Document.
- Hawaii parks may be able to incorporate recent studies gathered by Steve Lawson into NEPA work.
- Unlikely that Grand Canyon or Hawaii parks could use new/additional studies

 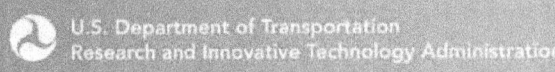

Use of Expert Advisory Group:
- Test hypotheses for future use
- Funding issues Visitor Experience
- Listening opportunity assessments may require more acoustic data

Next steps for review of acoustical work:
1) Step 1 Acoustician review work and
2) Step 2 Sociologists review work
3) Step 3 Volpe Center reviews work
4) Obtain estimates for review panel

Guidance for Researchers
- Results oriented research with thresholds in mind
- Danger of too narrowly focused work.
- 18 Month OMB Review process for Surveys – START NOW!
- Should create a "High Level" Roadmap to provide "shoulders" for future research

Analysis Plan
- Future plan
- Impact criteria
- Acquiring additional field data (OMB Requirements)
- Managing grants

Supplemental Materials (Recorded on Flip Charts from Technical Expert Break Out Session)

TECH EXPERT BREAKOUT
Questions from Technical Experts (contributors in parentheses):

1) How do we improve "generalizability" for management zones? (Nick)
2) How do motivations, values, and expectations influence response? (Bill)
3) What acoustical issues can we currently not assess from existing acoustical data? (Jim)
   a. Salience of acoustic metrics (indicators) for visitor response
4) What are the strengths & weaknesses of multiple methods? (Steve)
   a. Dose-response
   b. Audio clips
   c. In-situ
   d. Laboratory based
   e. Qualitative
   f. Observation
   g. Modeling
   h. Physiological?
5) What are the management and monitoring issues? (Bob)

TASK 1 – Research Priorities
a) Pre-meeting prep – KSN references
b) 3-day meeting
   a. Matrix with NPS soundscape zones and respective management goals
   b. Reanalysis design (high-level, dose-response)
   c. Priorities beyond reanalysis
c) Post meeting production
   a. White paper
   b. Roadmap

155

TASK 2 – Reanalysis of Existing Data
  a) Reanalyze
    a. Existing dose-response work
    b. Hawaii audio clips & listening
    c. Muir Woods program of research
    d. Yellowstone & Grand Teton listening
    e. Lab studies (Mace and Borrie)
  b) Draft and Final Report
  c) Meeting to present and discuss findings/next steps